STRAIGHT UP
& PERSONAL

Also by Don Cherry

STRAIGHT UP

The **WORLD** ACCORDING *to* **GRAPES**

& PERSONAL

ANCHOR CANADA

I thank you, God, for helping me survive.

Library and Archives of Canada Cataloguing in Publication has been applied for.

ISBN: 978-0-385-68110-0

Cover image: Phillip MacCallum / Stringer / Getty Images
Cover design: Five Seventeen
Printed and bound in the USA

Published in Canada by Anchor Canada,
a division of Random House of Canada Limited
A Penguin Random House company

www.penguinrandomhouse.ca

10 9 8 7 6 5 4 3 2 1

TABLE OF CONTENTS

STRAIGHT UP
& PERSONAL

LESSONS LEARNED

I AM IN THE WATER in the middle of the St. Lawrence River off Wolfe Island and drifting along with the current and waves, hanging on for dear life to a paddleboat. I've finally realized that circumstances I will explain later have me in a desperate situation. I know I cannot last much longer, as I am getting weaker and weaker. I look at the shore . . . it's too far, for I would never make it. But I've got to do something, as I know I cannot hang on much longer. As I drift along, strange thoughts enter my mind. If something did happen, I can see the headlines now: CBC SPORTSCASTER DROWNS IN THE ST. LAWRENCE. Some people would be happy, I am thinking, but let me tell you how I got into this nightmare.

That very morning, my wife, Luba, and I are sitting on the dock with our coffee, and one of the discussions is about me selling back to Gordon Bay Marine our Boston Whaler. I say to Luba, "I know you are not too happy about me selling the Whaler, but let's face it: we hardly use it." We had a paddleboat, which she used, and a canoe that a family member had left there, but nothing that could be used safely to save someone. Luba answers, "Yes, you are right, but I really think we should get a small rowboat or something in case somebody gets in trouble in the river. You never know. The St. Lawrence can be dangerous at times, and a storm can blow in any minute."

I answer, "Yes, someday we will get something."

That afternoon, about three o'clock, I am reading in bed and fall asleep, and suddenly I hear Luba calling my name, saying that the paddleboat has broken free from the shore and is drifting away. I suppose I have to get it. I remember we have the canoe that was behind the garage and I have never used the canoe or the paddle, so as I am pushing the canoe in the water, Luba says, "Wait I will get a life jacket."

I laugh. "Me wear a life jacket? No thanks." I paddle out to the middle of the river, and I notice the wind is picking up and it's getting rougher, but everything is going well, no problem. And as I look back now, I was getting too brave and too cocky and getting careless, not paying attention—which is a dangerous thing on the river. I can see that the paddleboat is caught in the current, and as the waves pick up, it's drifting away faster. But I finally catch up to the boat and tie the rope on the back of the canoe.

The wind has really picked up, but I am making progress back to the cottage, and for some strange reason I don't feel the boat is towing right, so I turn to undo the boat to retie it. That is when my troubles begin, as my paddle falls into the water. As I turn and bend over to retrieve the paddle, the canoe tips over and water starts rushing over the top of the canoe. I cannot stop it, and over I go into the water with the canoe upside down.

It is hard for me to describe the feeling when this happened. It was like, "Is this really happening?" and "Can this be real? These things happen to other people, not me; this can't be happening in the middle of the St. Lawrence." I look, and the canoe is hardly above water. I look the other way, and the paddleboat is fast drifting away. What to do? Stay with the canoe, which is bobbing almost under water, or take off after the paddleboat that is fast disappearing? I got to remember I can't panic. It's just a little swim, I say to myself. Don't get excited. I kick off my running shoes and take off after the boat; honest to God, my thoughts go to a fellow hockey player called Ross Lowe who played for Eddie Shore's Springfield Indians in the American Hockey League. I remembered we all looked up to him. It was my rookie year, 1954–55, and what a year Ross had. He had a tough time, knocked around hockey in the NHL Boston and Montreal and ended up in the graveyard of hockey, Springfield, with the Darth Vader of hockey, Eddie Shore, but he never quit, worked hard, and in 1955 in 60 games he got 32 goals and 50 assists and 82 points. He was a First Team All-Star and the MVP of the league and boy, was he tough.

Ross got a break when he was drafted by the New York Rangers and signed a big contract that year, and we all wished him well. What a break to get away from Shore and go to the Big Show—there's hope for all of us. Ross loved to fish, and being from Oshawa, he had lots of opportunities to fish. That summer, after being drafted by the New York Rangers on June, Ross was out in the lake on a hot day, and he decided to go for swim. Ross dove off the boat, and when he came up from the dive, he noticed the boat was drifting away. Ross took off after the boat, but the faster he swam, the faster the boat drifted away. Ross never made it to the boat and went under. Everybody assumed he drowned, but the rumour we heard was that he died of a heart attack from panic watching the boat drift away.

We all thought, "What a bad break, just when he was getting his big hockey break," but I'm not thinking of Ross's big break in hockey as I swim as hard as I can. I think of Ross drowning on account of panicking, so again I say, "Relax, it's just a little swim," and I calm down and swim slow but sure. I finally catch up with the boat and think my troubles are over, but they are just beginning. I look back at the dock in the distance and can make out Luba all by herself—what must she be thinking? I look around for a boat somewhere in the river to get rescued, but not one boat in sight. It's July—surely some boat will come along. But no fishing boat, no sailboats, nothing. The St. Lawrence is empty and the waves are picking up again and I'm drifting farther and farther away from shore.

I try to get into the boat, but it's so high. I can't climb aboard; I make a mistake and keep trying and trying and make myself very weak. As I try to hang on to the boat, I have to extend myself over the side of the boat and grab hold of the arm of the foot paddle. This is very awkward, contributing to my weakening condition. I'll give it one more try to get in and I'll go all out. I let go and give it my all and get my leg almost over, but being so weak I fall back in the water. I look and wonder if I can make the shore, as I am a pretty good swimmer, but I think of all the stories I have read when the guy, after a boat accident, tries for the shore and he drowns. I stay with the boat, thinking, "Oh why, oh why didn't I listen to Luba and take the life jacket?" Now I know why they are called life jackets. I know I cannot last much longer. I should never have weakened myself trying to get in the boat. A strange feeling comes over me. I think this could be it, and I am accepting it very calmly. I look up at the sky and think, "What a beautiful blue sky."

Meanwhile, Luba is at her wits' end; she's putting on a life jacket and is going to try to swim out to me and bring one for me, but a friend working at the back of the cottage, who came running when he heard her cries for help, stops her. He tells her, "That would be suicide" and "No sense both of you going down." Still no boats on the river, which is unbelievable. She calls around and no one is home except a farmer named Ken Murphy, and he starts to phone everyone along the shoreline to see if anyone can come out by boat to rescue me. I am drifting faster and faster away as the wind and the current are picking up and I am now in the middle of the current. I look at the beautiful blue sky and say, "Well, Lord, if this is the way it's going to be, then it's got to be." I am really getting weaker and weaker and I don't know how much longer I can hang on. I think I faintly hear a boat starting up in the distance and I say, "Lord, I hope it's for me." I know I have never heard such an amazing sound as I keep praying to let it be for me, let it be for me.

As the sound gets louder, I know it's for me and thank God. It's a gentleman called Al Doyle, who received the call from Ken Murphy. As Al glides up to me, he says, "Having a little trouble, Don?" and I answer, "A little." I find I am too weak to get into his boat, so I sit on a little platform beside the outboard motor, and as we start in, I notice the paddleboat and canoe floating away and I say, "Al, as long as we are here, why don't we pick up the canoe and the paddleboat?" He swings by the canoe and boat and I grab the ropes and we start in. It must be a strange sight, a guy sitting on a platform, towing two boats in. We make it to the dock. Al drops me off with the boats and waves goodbye, knowing how grateful I am. I am so embarrassed, and thankfully Luba never mentions the life jacket. She's so happy to have me back alive.

As I go to speak, a strange thing happens. I cannot speak; my mouth has gone dry. I later read the same thing happened to another person with a near-death experience—his mouth dried up also. I guess that's what fear does to you.

Sometimes, when I'm quietly sitting alone, many thoughts come to mind about that day, but there is one thing that comes to mind that seems to haunt me. I still get that gut sensation when I picture the canoe tipping over and the water pouring in. Feeling helpless and having no way of stopping it. There are times when I wake up in the middle of the night, dreaming of the water pouring in, and I say, "God, thank you for giving me a second chance at life."

Much to my embarrassment, the story got around Wolfe Island, and when I was asked about it by an old-timer who was a hockey nut, I answered him by saying, "Yeah, it was embarrassing that I would risk my life for a stupid paddleboat." He just shook his head and said to me, "You know the story of Babe Siebert?"

And I said, "I've heard of him. He played back in the thirties."

He says, "Check out his story."

I did check out Babe's story. His name was Albert "Babe" Siebert, of Zurich, Ontario. He was born in 1904 and played when he was young for Kitchener. He signed with the Montreal Maroons of the NHL in 1925 and won the Stanley Cup, believe it or not, in his first year. He was a big, tough winger. He was later traded to the New York Rangers and believe it or not, the Rangers won the Cup in his first year with them. He was traded to the Montreal Canadiens, put back on defence because they wanted him to be on the ice more. And believe it or not, as a defenceman, he won the Hart Trophy. He retired two years later and became coach of the Canadiens.

Babe was enjoying his summer at the cottage on Lake Huron and was looking forward to his first year as coach of the powerful Canadiens. Babe was on top of the world. He won the Stanley Cup, was a Hart Trophy winner and now was the coach of the famous Montreal Canadiens. What could be better? And he had a lovely wife and kids. But life, as we know, has twists and turns. While his wife was giving birth to his second child, she became paralyzed from the waist down. Most of Babe's salary from the Canadiens went to a nurse who cared for her. Babe's wife wanted to go to the games, and Babe carried her into the Forum before the game and people always saw him carrying her out after the game. They were deeply in love, but it must have been very tough stuff for the both of them.

Babe enjoyed his days at the cottage. One day, his wife and kids were at the cottage on Lake Huron. His kids were playing out on the lake, floating on the inner tube of a car, the way we all used to. Somehow the tube got away from the kids and started to drift away. Babe dived in and started to swim after the tube to retrieve it. But the tube kept drifting away, and Babe wouldn't quit. He kept going and going until he got tired. And he disappeared, with his children watching from the shore. It's tough to take. What a sad ending. Drowning while your wife and children were watching.

Times were tough now for his wife. In 1939, the NHL put on an All-Star game at the Forum and raised money for his widow. That's all I could find about Babe Siebert and his family. I often wonder how his family made out after his passing, because back then, the players had no pension. I hope God was kind. The family needed a break.

I saw the old-timer at the garage a couple of days later. I told him I knew the story of Babe Siebert. He looked at me and said, "The lesson is, enjoy life when you can. You never know what's waiting for you around the next corner."

* * *

I have been asked many times what player who should have been a star in the NHL threw it away on booze and drugs. Unfortunately, I could name a lot of guys, and it was sad to see guys with a lot of talent go down the drain. And there is nothing you can do to stop them. Some guys, at the end of their career, straighten out when they do something that shocks them into reality. One guy, who was a boozer, when drunk pushed his mother down on the floor. When his sister told him the next day what he had done, he quit cold turkey, which doesn't happen too often. A lot of guys try to kick the habit, and they do for a time, but usually after a while, they fall off the wagon. John Barleycorn is a tough guy to get rid of.

I must admit, and I'm not very proud of it, I drank a lot of beer in my playing time in the minors. It was the thing to do. It was strange when I was a rookie and I broke into the pros. I did not drink at all in my rookie year in Hershey, and that is where Boston had its training camp. I was twenty years old and never joined in with the boys when they would have a "session" after practice. I thought they were going to sit around and talk hockey, which they did, but along with the talk, plenty of suds went down the hatch. I have to say, as I sat there listening, not saying a word, as rookies did in those days, I noticed as the players drank, their feelings seemed to come out on their thoughts on different players. I have to say, it was their true feelings, and I saw many a player turn on one another. When they say "courage in a bottle," it's so true. Guys who wouldn't say a word all of a sudden become brave and, instead of being quiet, became bigmouths and went looking for trouble. In this atmosphere, they almost always found it, and when you heard, "Step outside and say that," the time had come.

It's funny: nobody ever tried to stop a fight unless the guy was a helpless drunk. I have seen some bloody fights. They only stopped when one guy went down. It was survival of the fittest back in those days. I also noticed that some guys could drink all day and you would never notice a difference. Other guys—two beers and they're flying. I learned as I got older, the guy to watch for was the guy who just sat there and never said a word, just looked, with that strange look in his eyes. It's true: still waters run deep.

When I was young, studying these guys, I noticed the sad spectacle of the guy who never knew when to stop, when he'd had too much. A lot of guys who never made it to the big time were bitter guys. The minor leagues and the beers did that to some guys. They figured they'd got the short end of the stick, and it was tough to hear their sad tales, but through it all, I sat there with my Coke. I would not have a beer, even with all the coaxing, till I turned professional.

I turned pro with the Boston Bruins in Hershey, so now I could be one of the boys. I must say I had a "taste of the honey," as the rich boys would say. My mother was dead-against drinking. We never had it in the house. She always said, "Never drink gin. It's in the blood." I never knew what she meant till the time we won the Memorial Cup with the Barrie Flyers. In junior, I never drank beer. At the house parties, everybody was drinking, which they should not be because we were all under twenty. "Come on, Don." "Don, don't be a party pooper." I remember a guy made me a Tom Collins (I'll never forget the name). Hey, it tasted like a grapefruit drink, so I had a couple of Tom Collinses, but with gin. I woke up the next day in the host's spare bedroom, feeling like I was dying. Now I knew what Mom meant by "it's in the blood." I never touched the "hard stuff" again, liquor of any kind.

But I must admit I fell into the routine. The routine went something like this: milkshake for breakfast; practice 10:00 A.M. to 11:30 A.M. (we had no off-ice training in those days); shower; lunch at our favourite restaurant, DeAngelo's, consisted of two eggs, bacon and toast; nap in the afternoon.

(I often wondered when, after I retired and had no job, and no trade and no money, why I didn't at least learn a trade in those off-hours. My little brother, Richard, who played for the Philadelphia Flyers and the Boston Bruins, as well as Providence and Oklahoma City, studied in his off-hours every minute of the week, even on long bus rides. He earned a teacher's certificate and studied at Queen's University and received his bachelor's degree and master's degree. He was set for life.)

Unfortunately, I have to admit I turned into one of the guys that I used to look down upon when I was a rookie and non-drinker. I will admit it was a hard life, but that's no excuse. We would play Friday, get on a bus and travel all night. Play Saturday, get on the bus right after the game, drive all the way back to Hershey and play Sunday night. Three games in three nights, injured or not. Treat your own injuries. I can't remember a time in sixteen years, anybody missing a game with the flu or a cold. You played unless you had a bone showing. With only six teams in the NHL, there were lots of guys to take your spot.

There was a lot of drinking after practice. I am now ashamed to say it was drinking, never eating. Just peanuts and popcorn, and some guys could go for ten hours. It was amazing and it was interesting to see the different ways guys could handle John Barleycorn.

I must admit I had a good time and I never got "blotto," that I can remember, and I was the only guy who would phone home and say where we were having our sessions— except once, just once, and it almost cost me a coaching job. Rose would give me a frosty answer when I would call, but never gave me heck. If the wives wanted to know where their husbands were, they would phone Rose.

I asked my teammates, "Why don't you phone your wives and tell them where you are in case there's an emergency?" Their answer was, "Look, when I get home, I'm going to catch hell. Why should I phone home and catch hell twice?"

I had a good friend, my best friend on the team, and it was getting to be that we were the last ones to leave, closing the place. Every time I would go to leave, he would get upset. Finally, I had to take a stand. He was very upset and called me names, but enough was enough. I didn't like the way we were heading. He was a good athlete—played many sports and won many championiships and awards. Why didn't he get a shot at the big time? Because he liked John Barleycorn too much. He lost everything—his lovely wife and children, a great career—but he is just like one of the many guys I knew back then whose careers were ruined by drinking. It was sad to see.

I remember in Rochester I played with Al Arbour and on defence with Larry Hillman. They would occasionally drop into our sessions, but would leave after one or two beers. As I look back now, both went on to play for the Stanley Cup, both turned into great coaches—Al winning the Stanley Cup and Larry winning the Avco Cup in the World Hockey Association. After playing many years in the AHL and looking back, I guess it's not too surprising, and it tells you something about us, why we drank so much. I had to say a lot of us were bitter about not making the show, but I feel that's just an excuse. I guess we were having a good time, not thinking of the future. I will admit most of us stopped the life of drinking once we retired and got away from each other, and I will admit I missed it badly—the camaraderie and fun were gone. Little did we know it was for our own good. Some guys never stopped, and it was their undoing.

The alcoholic will never stop unless he wants to, no matter what you do. "The taste is there," as my mother used to say. I tried to help guys, but it never worked out. When I was coach and GM of the Rochester Americans, I signed a guy I knew was an alkie. How did I know? I played and roomed with him, so I knew what I was getting into. He was a dandy defenceman, but couldn't leave the stuff alone. Red flags were all over the place, but I was a young GM. I should have signed him till Christmas, and if he didn't straighten out, let him go, but I felt sorry for him and his lovely family, and he was such a lovable guy when sober. The guys loved him when he was sober, but the signing was not fair to our owners. They trusted me and I let them down. I feel that way, even though they made a couple hundred thousand dollars that year.

When I was his roommate (and that was a treat), one time he broke curfew and came in late, drunk as a lord. I was so pissed I went into the bathroom and left the window open so he would freeze. He turned purple, but got up the next morning feeling fine. I caught a cold.

He used to tell me about his escapades. The bosses put up with him when he was young because he was such a great prospect. One time, he told me, he was playing for Tulsa in the Central League, and they were on the road, and as usual, after the game (which his team lost), his coach put a curfew on. Curfew meant nothing to this guy; they

were made to be broken. This time, they were warned: anybody out, it was trouble. Big time. So he told me he was
going to be in on time, but one beer led to another and he
said, "What the heck?" So he and a buddy are in a strip club
at one end of the bar, and who should walk in and stand at
the end of the bar? The team management. The two players
ducked down and hid, but how to get out? He knows he's in
deep trouble, as he's been caught before and warned. One
more time and that's it. So he looks around and sees the
entrance to the stage is right beside him and they're getting
ready to start the show, but he figures if he runs across the
stage he can get across before they open the curtains. So he
sneaks up the stairs, he runs across the stage, and as he's a
tall guy, he smacks his head on a beam and is knocked out
cold. The music starts, the curtains open, the team management look up from the bar and see their star player spread-
eagle, out cold, on the strippers' stage.

I could see I wasn't going to help him in Rochester, and
he was disrupting the team, so I told him not to come to the
arena—stay home. "If anybody asks, just say you're hurt." I
told the press he had an injury. I paid him. I could have just
cut him, which I should have done, to be fair to the owners,
but I was young and stupid. But you know, if it had happened again, I'd do the same thing.

The end is not happy. He and his wife, who also was an
alcoholic, lost their two beautiful children, and I never
heard of them again.

I have not mentioned his name. What's the point? You
just hurt Mom and Dad and relatives. I am going to tell you
about who, to me, is the biggest disappointment and talent

wasted that was ruined by the "taste." He was a beauty player, big—six foot two—fearless, skated like the wind, magic with the puck, a slapshot you would die for, he had it all. A phenom, as they say. He even broke Bobby Orr's record for goals and Denis Potvin's record for points by a defenceman. Listen to this: in junior hockey: 60 games, 47 goals, 108 assists. Imagine, 155 points in 60 games. He went high in the draft to Quebec in 1987, ahead of Joe Sakic. He had the world on a string; everybody thought this guy is going to be in the NHL a long time. Although I must admit, I had heard a few rumours about him, that he liked the high life. What the heck, we thought, he's just a young guy having fun, but we thought wrong. The rumours were true. Surely he would straighten out with all that money to be made. He never did.

It got worse. He had such great talent, everybody wanted him. They thought they could straighten him out. Listen to the teams he went to: Quebec Nordiques in the NHL, Halifax, New Haven, Muskegon, Pittsburgh, Cleveland, Atlanta, Las Vegas, Kansas City, Montreal, Minnesota, Detroit in the IHL, Davos in the Swiss League, Kansas City again, Milan 24 in Italy, Germany. He was running out of countries.

I remember he was put as a roommate with another player who was also hooked on drugs and such. I often wonder the reason. Maybe they thought if one boy saw how the other acted, he would stop? (By the way, the roommate died a violent death at the hands of the police when they tried to arrest him.) Or the team just thought, "Hey, they're both lost causes, let's just put them together and not upset the rest of the team." Either way, they were doomed. He was once found naked in a high school kitchen, covered in cooking oil, where he was arrested. He did try to straighten out, got married, but while on vacation he died of a heart attack.

It's got to be one of the saddest stories in sport. Movie-star looks, breaking records in hockey, he went from the toast of hockey to having it all end at the age of thirty-two.

I know what you're thinking: "Why dwell on these stories? What's the point?" I have a reason. A lot of junior players and younger kids not in hockey will read this book. That is why there is no profane language in the book again. I know what you're thinking: "Are you kidding? The kids could teach you a few." Maybe you're right. Maybe one or two kids reading the stories of these guys will smarten a few guys up. "And if they're asked at a party to smoke a joint, what's the harm?" I tell the story of the heartbreak of two parents who wrote to me about their son who was a young hockey player, who, while at a hockey tournament, was late for the bus. The coach came to his room to get him and saw a joint in his room. It wasn't even his, but he wouldn't tell whose it was. The coach suspended him there and then from the team. The team went and played the game. When they came back, his roommate found he had committed suicide by hanging himself with his belt. Naturally his mom and dad were heartbroken. They would give anything to get their son back, and they wanted to get the word to other kids. No matter what you do, your real friends will forgive you and so will your mom and dad.

I know, reader, that these are depressing stories, but if it can save one kid, I feel it's worth it.

* * *

Hazing in sports has been going on since sports have existed. Rookies are the targets. It starts with rookies picking up the pucks after practice, carrying the bags for the trainers, cleaning the bus up after a long trip (in the juniors and minors). It graduates from there, where it gets meaner—shaving of private parts, etc.

My first experience with hazing was when I was away at sixteen to play for the Barrie Flyers in the Ontario Hockey Association. The vets were always discussing whether one guy could lift three guys. I thought it was impossible. There was a rookie in the club who thought he was hot stuff, and he said to the vets that it "can't be." They said, "Okay, after practice, we'll show you."

After practice, we all showered and were naked. The vets said, "We need three guys on the floor, laying on their backs." Meanwhile, everyone was betting, including Hot Stuff. So the vets said, "We got two guys on the floor. We need a third. How about you, Hot Stuff? You get in the middle." He got in the middle and they were told to entwine their legs and arms around each other so the one guy could lift the three of them.

Hot Stuff was in the middle, and the guy was lifting said, "Now, can anybody move?" All three said no. "Okay, he's ready!" Four guys came out dressed as barbers, with towels and razors and soap, and proceeded to shave around the private parts of Hot Stuff.

When I was coaching Colorado, the players just happened to pick the day the owner from New Jersey, Arthur

Imperatore, came to visit the club as their day for hazing. Unbeknownst to me, as we're talking by a dressing room, the owner looks in, and here we have eighteen naked guys shaving another naked guy. Imperatore didn't understand, and it was hard to explain the ritual to him. He was not happy.

When I was in Sudbury, we had an American trainer who was a rookie. I knew the players were going to get him, so I took him aside and said, "Look, the players are going to haze you someday. Just go along with it. Don't fight them."

"Oh yeah? They better not try that stuff on me."

I said, "Okay, it's your funeral. Ya can't fight eighteen guys."

Sure enough, after practice one day, they got him—and he did fight back. He put up a good fight, but they broke his arm. Ya can't win against eighteen guys.

When I was in Rochester, there was a guy, the most obnoxious little rookie ever. If he wasn't playing, he'd phone his agent. It was like he'd been in the league for years. I knew sooner or later they'd get him. Sure enough, in a hotel room after a game, they grabbed him. Now, this guy had lovely hair. It was his pride and joy, always blow-drying, gel, so instead of shaving his crotch, they shaved half of his head. He went nuts crying, threatening to sue us, take us to court. Funny thing is, while this was going on, the coach walked by the room, looked in, had an idea of what was going on, and kept on walking. He was happy this stiff was getting his, as they say.

I know some people say it's an initiation and some of it I liked, it was fun, like lifting three guys. But some of it was just mean, and to tell you the truth, I never really liked it.

The one hazing incident I really felt bad about was at the Springfield Indians training camp. It concerned a young player who was at our camp, whose father played in the NHL, and he really thought he was somebody. I knew his time was coming—not if, but when. Sure enough, after practice, they went to grab him. He made the mistake of fighting them. He was a big, strong guy and it was touch and go. They wrestled around the dressing room. Unfortunately for him, the room had red-hot radiators on the wall. As they were wrestling, he was held against the hot radiator, which burned his back and bum. It was so bad you could see the rivets from the radiator on his skin. They didn't care and showed no mercy, held him down and put some ointment on him, which was blue. They covered his whole body in it and it would not come off. As I was leaving the arena, I looked into the shower, where the kid was showering, trying to get the stuff off. It was not coming off. He looked up and saw me and said, "You know what's the worst about this, Grapes? I was just married. Imagine, I have to go home looking like this." As I left, I heard him sobbing.

I guess all this hazing started in the English schools, and I know it was just as tough in the U.S. Marines. They want to know if you're tough enough to be a marine. Same thing in baseball, and definitely in football, to see if you can stand the gaff, as they say.

I've noticed one thing over the years: I never ever saw a tough guy rookie hazed. There could be a lot of reasons why, but I feel the reason they don't haze tough guys is you might get the tough guy today—like I said, you can't beat eighteen guys—but there's always tomorrow and there won't be eighteen guys around. And besides, in hockey, you might need that tough guy when the going gets rough.

I was never hazed, and I will state now that I never liked hazing. I saw a couple of guys never recover from the hazing. There was only one hazing I loved, when they shaved the head of the guy in Rochester. We all liked it, especially when the little rat cried.

* * *

I remember my very first "bad," as they say, write-up. I had been on TV for a year. I call the first year on TV the honeymoon—the press don't know you, so they leave you alone. Then, if you get successful, it's when the dogs come out. It's funny. Down in the States, it's not like that. You can sort of feed on your success—in the States, they say "go for it." Now, if you're no good, they show no mercy. But in Canada, if you're successful, it's your turn. It happened to Ron MacLean when he started out on *Hockey Night in Canada*. Young guy from Red Deer, Alberta. He was good, make no mistake. I kept telling him, "You're on your honeymoon." He didn't understand. He asked, "What are you talking about, I'm on a moon?" I laughed. "You'll see," said I.

Ron's honeymoon ended, of all places, in Calgary, Alberta, at the All-Star Game in 1985. Ron was the host of the All-Star banquet. He did his usual great job and he was feeling pretty good till he picked up the paper the next day. He was ripped to shreds in the paper. His honeymoon was over; he was crushed. His first bad write-up—in his hometown, of all places. When I saw him, I said, "Welcome to the club!"

My first rip job was done by a distinguished sportswriter by the name of Trent Frayne. He was the winner of many awards and was well thought of. I thought his columns were great. But boy, after a "Coach's Corner," he gave it to me, both barrels. I forget what it was about, but I was in shock. Honestly, I didn't know if I could go back on TV. It took me a couple of weeks to get over it. The executive producer, Ralph Mellanby, laughed and said, "Forget about it, this is a tough business, and to survive, you've got to be tough. If you can't take it, get out of the business. You'll get a lot of write-ups like that before you're through. Forget it."

I thought, "Easy for him to say." But after a month, I gradually came out of the shock. Then another beauty write-up came out. This one had my picture, and under it, the reporter listed what I was, just the names:

"Neanderthal." I had to ask somebody, "What is a Neanderthal?" "A big, tough caveman who carries a club." I thought, "Hey, that's not too bad."

"Troglodyte." It's a little dwarf that lives under a bridge and is evil.

"Misogynist." A fear of women.

I looked these up in the dictionary. And then there were the usual names—evil, etc. My second bad write-up. It didn't hurt quite as much, and the next bad one didn't hurt as much as the second. My hide was getting thicker. It was pretty hard to hurt me after a while. One guy went below the belt and said, "Do you ever notice when Don Cherry gets in trouble, he always puts on kids with cancer?" Nice, eh? But like I said, I got tough. Ralph was right. "Can't stand the heat? Stay out of the kitchen."

The Montreal *Gazette* in particular had it in for me. It all started in the eighties. Ron MacLean had told the kids that were going to be drafted by the NHL that he would get them on TV on *Hockey Night in Canada*. So the kids got haircuts, new suits, shoes shined. The came into the studio and Ron said, "Sorry, guys. We don't have time," which happens a lot on TV. The kids were heartbroken. They had told their parents and friends to look for them on TV. I argued with Ron, but it was impossible. It wasn't his fault. I said, "Okay, we'll put them on 'Coach's Corner.'" I told them to come back at the start of the first period. That's when I started to put the prospects on "Coach's Corner," a tradition that has been going on now for twenty years.

I noticed there were only four kids at the time when we did "Coach's Corner." I wondered where the other three were. The paper the next day said: "Cherry proves he is a bigot because he didn't put the three French kids on his segment at 'Coach's Corner,' only the English kids." The paper was right. I only put on the English kids because the French kids, at the time "Coach's Corner" was on, were being introduced and honoured as prospects for the NHL at centre ice in the Forum. I thought that was the best. The Forum was introducing the French kids, not the English. I was going to put on the whole seven on "Coach's Corner," and now *I* was called the bigot.

The Montreal *Gazette* has a writer named Jack Todd, an American who had it in for me from day one. It started in the early eighties, and he never let up. Jack had a write-up last year around the time Rogers took over *Hockey Night in Canada* and, for a while, it looked like I wasn't coming back. Remember how the boss at Rogers said at the press conference, when asked if I was coming back, "We are evaluating everybody"? The last two times I was fired, the boss said, when asked the same question, "We're evaluating Cherry." And the next day, gonzo. So Jack did this write-up the next day, it was so good. It got into Canadian Press and email or whatever they do to spread the word. Bobby Orr phoned me about the column the next day, so I know it went all over the States and Canada. Jack started out with his opening line: "I've spent half a career arguing with Don Cherry. I've hated him longer than some of you have been alive." He goes on:

> You know how it is: I'm one of those lefty kook tree huggers he's always snarling about and he's one of those pigheaded, narrow-minded, right-wing bullies I've been battling since fourth grade.
>
> Cherry's noisy support for Rob Ford? Eeesh. The maudlin way he wraps himself in the mantle of Canada's Armed Forces (a trick borrowed by Stephen Harper and Peter MacKay) even though, like Harper and MacKay, he never served? Double eeesh.
>
> But I want to say this, loud and clear: If the Don is turfed from *Hockey Night in Canada*, I'll miss him. Because Cherry belongs on *Hockey Night in Canada*. *Hockey Night in Canada* belongs on the CBC. And the CBC belongs to us.
>
> If Cherry had been fired from within *HNIC* as it existed until Tuesday, that's one thing. But if he's to be jettisoned by a big private corporation in pursuit of

eventual control over the entire CBC network, that's something else.

Perhaps that seems like an exaggerated response to Tuesday's announcement of the 12-year, $5.2-billion deal between the NHL and Rogers Communications. I don't think so. The scariest words I heard Tuesday came from one of the Rogers suits (sorry, I didn't get the license plate) when he said something to the effect that "we look forward to future partnerships with the CBC."

("Partnership"? That's a good one. As partnerships go, the deal with *Hockey Night in Canada* is strictly of the "me master, you slave" variety.)

What worries me is that the brutally one-sided take-over of *Hockey Night in Canada* will become the wedge that leads to the eventual privatization of the CBC. Given that the deal also creates a horizontal and vertical monopoly for Rogers, you'd think the toothless CRTC might have something to say about it because monopolies are, by definition, bad for consumers — but expecting the CRTC to protect your interests is like asking a Great Dane to look out for your steak.

When I saw Gary Bettman and Rogers CEO Nadir Mohamed chortling and pumping hands Tuesday, I got queasy. It was like watching a couple of car salesmen congratulating each other after they've just taken some poor schnook on a deal for a used Ford Pinto.

Because we're that schnook and you just know that in the long run, we're going to get taken. In the words of the old country song, they get the gold mine, you get the shaft.

What's going to stand in Rogers's way? Not much. They now own *HNIC*: lock, P.J. Stock and barrel. Given that our wretched PM would love to kill the CBC, Cherry is perhaps the only person in this country with the juice to prevent the death of *Hockey Night in Canada* four years from now and eventually, perhaps, even the demise of the CBC itself.

Why? Like it or not, Cherry is more than just Don the Broadcaster, Don the Loudmouth, that SOB Don or even Don the Institution. He's a national symbol. If Rogers can tear him down, then nothing is safe.

If you want to know why the Rogers deal is so alarming, the fate of former Leafs GM Brian Burke is instructive. Burke worked for Rogers (and Bell) as an employee of MLSE. He was fired, not because he was a terrible GM, but because he ruffled the feathers of the suits. He wasn't the kind of yes-man they require.

Eventually, if Rogers or Bell or some other private entity takes over the CBC, this is how it's going to be. The bosses will claim (as they did Tuesday) that they won't tell their employees what to say. And it will be true — because they won't have to. Consciously or sub-consciously, the journalists will censor themselves. So long, public network with something other than the corporate interest at heart.

Cherry is a bulwark against all that, simply because of his sheer, critical mass. Love him or loathe him, we watch him every Saturday night, in all his fluorescent, megawatt, wardrobe-by-Liberace, ungrammatical, name-mangling, xenophobic glory.

After hockey itself, our second favourite national pastime might be arguing about Don Cherry. The debate tends to obscure an essential truth at the core of the Cherry phenomenon: The man is a superb, instinctive broadcaster, a master of the sound bite. Cherry doesn't attract attention, he compels it. He alone can compel enough attention to shine a light on the nastier aspects of this deal.

The suits from Rogers did not say that Cherry would be shown the door during that daylong drum roll that accompanied the announcement Tuesday—but they pointedly avoided saying that he would be retained.

Cherry's fate is important because, beyond all the justifiable carping about the increasingly amateurish *HNIC* production, I believe profoundly in the CBC itself, and I always have.

It's a pity that this deal comes at a time when the *HNIC* broadcasts are so badly in need of a revamp. Ron MacLean's influence has been disastrous, P.J. Stock has to go and the entire production needs an infusion of talent to bring it up to the industry standard set by TSN.

There are good people at *HNIC* who should be retained—Jim Hughson, Kevin Weekes, Cassie Campbell-Pascall, Garry Galley and especially Elliotte Friedman, who is one of the best hockey broadcasters in the country.

The real key to the whole package, however, is Don Cherry, AKA Grapes—because if he goes, then *HNIC* and possibly even the CBC itself are living on borrowed time.

It was sad to see the man, looking old and tired without his makeup Tuesday, asking reporters at a book-signing event, "Do I still have a job?"

We need to speak out, loud and clear: "Ya mess wit' Grapes, fellas, and you're messin' wit' us."

It's funny, what he said about me looking "old, tired without [my] makeup, asking reporters at a book-signing event, 'Do I still have a job?'" He was so right. I saw myself on the news that night, and I thought, "Man, you look like this is your last day." But let me tell you about my day that day. I had scheduled, unfortunately, everything on the day that Rogers bought hockey, including *HNIC*. I had to do interviews all morning, no lunch, took an hour at the Rogers press conference, where I found out I was being "evaluated," did a signing that afternoon, had to come down to the Air Canada Centre—we got stuck in traffic, got there late—had to do a signing and go upstairs to the bar and do TV interviews on the *Rock 'Em, Sock 'Em* video and pose for pictures with people. I was so tired that, for the first time ever, I had to say enough.

Go downstairs, and as I go out, there are ten TV stations, radios, newspapers. As I attempted to do the interviews, the guy from CTV's batteries run out. I said, "Hurry up, we will wait." Finally get going, asking me questions. I have no answer, as the Rogers buy was a surprise to everybody. I go home, switch on the TV, and there I am looking like "the wrath of God," as my mother used to say.

I have to say, this column, even with words like "pig-headed," "narrow-minded," "right-wing bully," "wardrobe by Liberace," "ungrammatical," "name-mangling" and "xeno-phobic glory [I know my buddies are wondering about that one—I looked it up in the dictionary and it means dislike, hatred, fear of strangers or aliens]," it was totally unexpected to have him want me to stay. I thought he would be cheering for my departure. Life is funny. The guy who has been taking shots at me for thirty years is the only one who wrote that I should stay. Who would have thought?

* * *

When I do those walk-ins before the games on Hockey Night in Canada, I never know what to expect. I try not to be seen just before I go in. We did not plan it right last year, for Hockey Day in Canada in Lloydminster, Saskatchewan. As we drove up before I made my entrance, I told the driver and the PR guy to park a block from the arena and wait for the call to the front of the arena for my big entrance. Unfortunately, we drove up to the parking lot and turned the car around; now everybody could see me and everybody wanted a picture or an autograph. Normally, no problem, but I had little time to make my entrance and had to think of what to say. The PR guy got out and said, "I will tell them no autographs." I was furious. He didn't realize I'm the guy who looks bad if he stops them. They'll think, "Look at him, a big shot. Too busy for pictures or autographs."

We got the call: thirty seconds, start your way in. We have to be on the minute for TV. I arrive at the front like a big shot; it was so embarrassing. Opened the door by the Mounties and started in. If you notice, I only slap everybody's hands. I'll tell you why. On the way through the gauntlet, I used to shake hands. Once, as I shook this old guy's hand, he held on and crushed my hand and wouldn't let go. I literally had to pry my hand off with my other hand. Another time, a little boy was dressed exactly like me in one of my flashiest jackets. His mom had gone to Fabricland and got the material and made his jacket. It was just luck that I was wearing the same jacket. He went to centre ice with me. A young man with a white English bull terrier greeted me. I took him on the ice, too.

I felt bad on my entrance in Lloydminster. I was very rude. It was a hectic time. Let me explain, as I have said you have to have it timed on the nose. As Ron is introducing me, I have to be coming on the ice. I can't have the Mounties or the police in front of me, as they slow me down. This girl was walking in front of me—she was the security, wearing a headset and all that. Well, as Ron was introducing me, she stopped dead in front of me and I couldn't get by. It was dark, and I couldn't see where I was stepping. I heard Ron and his intro, and I was still in the dark with three million viewers wondering where I was. Finally, I pushed her out of the way and said, "Get out of the way."

I can't believe I was so rude. When I got back home, I saw some of the video and wondered what she and her family must be thinking. Here she is, a volunteer, and I do a thing like that. I got her name and number and phoned her, hoping I would get her answering machine (I bet you've phoned a few times, hoping you would get the answering machine), but she answered. We had a long talk, and as she was hanging up, she said a nice thing: "Thanks for caring."

Remember I said earlier about parking in the parking lot and people waiting for an autograph? As I sat there, ticked off, I saw this dad and two young sons, about four and seven years old. It looked like they'd been there a long time. Finally, I couldn't take it any longer. I got out in my shirtsleeves and pointed for them to come to the car. I signed their programs, pictures and pucks and posed for a picture. The dad said, "Gee, Grapes, we didn't expect this. We've been waiting for two hours, hoping to see you." They didn't even have tickets to the game. As the call came—"Thirty seconds"—I happened to see out of the corner of my eye the dad and his two boys walking away. They were jumping around, doing high fives. I said to myself, "Life is good."

* * *

Just a few weeks ago, after I'd already written this story for the book, I got this letter:

Dear Mr. Cherry,

I would like to take the time to personally thank you for your kind gesture during the Hockey Day in Canada event held at the Lloydminster Exhibition grounds. My son, nephew and I waited around in anticipation of meeting you and getting your autograph. When we were asked by the arena staff to move from where we were standing, the boys and I were quite disappointed that meeting you probably wasn't going to happen. When we were leaving we noticed your SUV pull in and park, so we waited at the entrance of the parking lot in the hope of meeting you. When your assistant came over to get our items to be autographed, we could not have been happier. However, when you stepped out of the SUV and called us over, it was the opportunity of a lifetime.

Meeting fans for you is a daily occurrence, but to those two young boys, the impression that you left on them will last a lifetime. After you signed our items and were walking away, those boys were on cloud nine and couldn't wait to get home to share their experience. Since then, my son has taken the hat you signed to school to show anyone and everyone who will look.

Thank you again for going your of your way on a Saturday to make a lifetime memory for the three of us.

Sincerely,
Dion Kneller

* * *

I've often watched those investigative TV programs, and I've always had a thought that a little more is happening here than meets the eye. I found that out firsthand and it had to do with a cold remedy I was promoting called Cold-FX. Let me tell you how I became involved with Cold-FX. When I was young, I had asthma, and through the years I had multiple colds. I was in Edmonton doing *HNIC*—with a cold, as usual. I read where Glen Sather, the GM of the Edmonton Oilers, told his players to start taking Cold-FX for colds. Says I to myself, "If it's good for the players, it's good for me." So I took it for a year, and it works. A rep at Cold-FX was talking to Ron MacLean, and Ron said you should speak to Don, he takes it all the time. Long story short, I became the spokesman.

I heard through the grapevine that a TV station was going to investigate Cold-FX—whether it works, etc. I get a call about meeting the female investigator. I am in, says I. The investigation was pathetic. For instance, in a sloppy manner, they were asking teenagers about Cold-FX—whether it works, etc.,—and then they showed that the ginseng that's in Cold-FX came from China. The woman investigator starts on me. Now, she is used to people that are not on TV and she bullies them. Little does she know this is my world. In the conversation, she keeps bringing up the name of the president of Cold-FX, who has sold the company. I sense she doesn't know this. I said, "You keep bringing up the name of the president. You know she sold the company two years ago?" I got her.

I don't let up, no mercy. How can you call yourself an investigative program and not know the president of the company has been gone two years? How can anyone believe anything you say? I never let up. Now she's frustrated, and now I am leaving (this is on TV). The weasel who has the camera is going to tape me leaving as if I'm guilty and running away. All the while, I'm saying this on camera. Now, I'm telling you producers: if you make me look bad on the program, I will bury you, and you better do your homework before you get into a debate with me.

I see the program; naturally, they were okay with me, but they ambushed the president as she was getting into the car. She says, "I have no comment" (seeing as she sold the company two years ago), but on TV it looks like she has something to hide and looks guilty. That's how they work. So when you see all these programs that investigate, remember: take it all with a grain of salt.

* * *

When I meet people in the airports or on the streets and in general, I'm often asked what comment I've made on "Coach's Corner" has drawn the most reaction from people. "Is it when you called the Winnipeg Jets' [assistant] coach Alpo Suhonen dog food? Or when you said Pekka Rautakallio was as yellow as a duck's foot? When you said at the Chicago All-Star Game, when asked to comment about the people burning the U.S. flag over protests of the Gulf War, 'How come these kooks are always protesting and burning flags during the afternoon? Don't they ever work?' When you called someone who didn't agree with you on fights 'pukes'? When you and Ron MacLean argued whether Canada should have gone and helped the U.S. in the Gulf War and I remember the CBC couldn't stop you and Ron? Or when you had your picture taken with a female bull terrier in an Edmonton sweater and you said, 'That bitch didn't mean anything to me.' Or when the French got mad at you about the visor statement and you got booed by the Bloc in Parliament?"

I could go on, but it would be none of these incidents. The comment I made on CBC that brought the most reaction in thirty years is the one I made about how I don't believe women should go into men's dressing rooms. I said if men aren't allowed in women's dressing rooms, why should women be allowed in the men's dressing rooms? But actually, the last statement, about men in women's dressing rooms . . . I don't believe in either, I just said that. But the statement brought more reaction than any statement in thirty years. And this is the honest truth: more women have come up to me and said, "By the way, I agree that women should not be in the dressing room." Which surprised me.

The reason I don't like women in men's dressing rooms is the way that some men act. Remember, I said some *men* act. My reaction was triggered by a write-up in one of the papers about a woman reporter who was doing an interview with a basketball player, and in the background another basketball player had grabbed a long piece of Styrofoam, stuck it between his legs and was dancing around. This is tame compared to what I have seen at some times. Some guys actually walked around without a towel around them, just for kicks. And other things I'm not going to mention.

I said, "I would not want my daughter to be in the dressing room." Well, the reaction was predictable. The women reporters took offence, naturally. I knew that was coming. The left-wing papers had editorials, and I was called a redneck and a character and all that stuff.

They even had a voice from the past come at me in the form of a woman reporter named Robin Herman—the first female sports reporter for the *New York Times*. She had the headline: "Don Cherry, you were my hero." Robin was twenty-three when she was given the assignment of covering the New York Islanders. She says she remembers me fondly in those early days: "*You* were the first coach in the NHL to allow me, a female, accredited sports reporter and member of the Professional Hockey Writers' Association, into your locker room as a matter of policy. You were coaching the 'Big Bad Bruins,' and it was ironic that a team with that reputation should be the most forward-thinking in the NHL. Your PR man par excellence, Nate Greenberg, had persuaded you this was the way to go. . . . He and you were gentlemen. . . . The times they were a-changin' then, and the Bruins organization was smart enough to realize it. You should be proud of what you did. . . . I faced a draconian deadline of 11 P.M. . . . Every minute spent waiting for a team official to bring a player out of the locker room to speak to me separately in some dank hallway was excruciating."

I do remember Nate coming up to me after the game on Long Island and saying, "If this young girl doesn't get her story in by 11 P.M., she could lose her job." As there were a few fights that night, it was close to eleven at the time. I had other things on my mind. We had lost to the lowly Islanders and GM Harry Sinden was furious. We were a first-place team, and I and Harry Sinden and the team thought we blew the game and we were not properly prepared for the game. And it is my job to prepare them. I knew I was in trouble. I was listening to Harry tell me the team was not ready, etc., etc., and all the while, reporters were asking me questions. It was a hectic time.

As usual, after the game and in the midst of all this, Nate whispered to me and introduced me to a young female reporter and said something about her losing her job if she didn't get an interview or something and asked if she was all right to go into the dressing room. I was listening to Harry and said, "Yeah, yeah, go on in." I never thought anything of it. Later, Nate said thanks and I said, "For what?" Little did I know that Robin had been pleading with various team officials and the league itself for the better part of a year to let her in the dressing room and now I had opened the gates.

When we were in Boston, a female reporter came to me and said I let a female into the dressing room in New York and I said, "I did?" And they said, "Yes, and we're expecting the same treatment here in Boston." I'm done. I've opened up Pandora's box. *Now* I remember this. Beautiful woman reporter now expected to go into the room. There's no turning back now, and in they go. Everything seemed to go smoothly for a while, till one night after the game, Jean Ratelle—a perfect Jean Béliveau type, quiet and dignified, a classy gentleman, a Lady Byng Trophy winner—came to me and quietly closed the door and said, "I don't want to make trouble, but to have women in the dressing room is very upsetting to me and I'm not used to it. I protest against it." Jean was one of my favourites—like I said, a Jean Béliveau type. What to do?

I also found out that some of the wives were very unhappy with this situation. I came up with this idea: I said to the TV reporters and women writers, "Tell you what: I will give you any player you want after the game, the #1 star, anybody. I will bring them to you in my office for you and have a private interview. I will hold a press conference in the hall, and you get the first choice of any player." Thank goodness they went along with it. The guy reporters weren't too happy, but what the heck? They had me. What more could you want?

So, when did I change my mind about female reporters in the room? It started when players from other teams were acting up when female reporters were in the dressing rooms. I must admit that I wasn't happy with the way a couple of my players were acting, till I straightened them out. I know it's a little different now. Guys don't go directly into the dressing room naked when other reporters are in, but still act up—for example, the basketball players. And I repeat: I still don't want my daughter in a room with men with towels around them, fooling around. Let me ask you: Would you like your daughter in that room? I think not.

* * *

I will always remember when I was laid off from my construction job at Kodak in Rochester. It was not an easy time; I had no trade experience (unless you count operating a jackhammer a trade). I was a beast of burden, no education and no job, painting for two dollars an hour, working eight hours for sixteen dollars. One day, I got a call from a teammate who was forming a hockey school (let's call him Jim Smith). He asked if I'd like to be one of the instructors for a hundred dollars a week. Would I? I was the happiest guy in the world. I'd be there with bells on.

Monday morning, I'm there an hour early to get the kids checked in. Jim shows up fifteen minutes before the first session, but I already have everything straightened out. Kids are anxious—so am I. Jim has hired some players from the Rochester Americans. They show up five minutes before the session—obviously, they had a party the night before and are a little hungover. The session begins. I am gung ho! The players are struggling to get through the morning with the hangover. Lunch comes from twelve to one—I brown-bag it and am ready to go at one o'clock. The players show up at one-fifteen. I think they had a liquid lunch. I shoot pucks all day. I think I'm getting blisters because I haven't shot at goalies in a year. At the end of the day, I take off my gloves and my hands are bleeding from blisters. I can hardly drive home—I put tape on the blisters and drive mostly with my wrist.

I get home, and I am hurting. Rose suggests that she read somewhere that Epsom salts would be good. I go along with her and put my hands in Epsom salts. I think my head will explode with the pain. I try to wash the stuff off in our bathtub, but the faucet handles don't work.

The next day, I know, is not going to be fun, but I suck it up. It's a long way from your heart, as the old trainers in the AHL used to say.

We now have broken up the sessions. I'll take the first session and let the Americans players sleep in because it's party time. I have from eight to ten in the morning. Ten o'clock comes, and the players are late. I fill in for them for fifteen minutes and they stagger in (meanwhile, my hands are killing me—I keep opening up the blisters).

The whole week, the players are late and I fill in till they come on the ice. I have to take charge, and I give them a lecture. After that, they're on time. Now, you must remember, I'm just an instructor. It's called the Jim Smith Hockey Camp. We are in day five and Jim Smith has not been on the ice once, and kids keep asking me when Mr. Smith's coming on the ice. Jim was a pretty famous guy in Rochester. He has played most of his career there and he is a 40-goal scorer, but so far no show on the ice. I've got to be a little careful—this is not my school, I'm happy to get the hundred bucks—but this is not right. The kids are being cheated. Something has to be done, although I'll probably lose my precious hundred bucks.

I go into his office, and he just happens to be counting the kids' money, which makes me see red; but control yourself, Don, I say to myself. Think of the hundred.

Don: "Jim, the kids were asking when you're coming on the ice."

Jim: "Great!"

Don: "Jim, this is not right. It's your school, your name's on it, the kids are looking forward to seeing you and your great shot. Don't you think it would be nice to make an appearance these last two days?"

Jim: "It's none of your business."

Don: "Well, I'm making it my business."

Jim: "You know, Cherry, I give you a break and now you give me a hard time. Do you ever think that's why you can't get a job?"

(I've got to admit, folks, that hit home, but as my dad used to say, "In for a penny, in for a pound.")

Don: "Yeah, maybe you're right. I don't have a job, and I am having a hard time, but I'll tell you one thing: I don't try to cheat twelve-year-old kids. Now, get your skates on and get your ass on that ice."

He goes to say something, but thinks better of it. He goes on the ice, the kids love it and he is a hero.

This is my last day. He only gives me sixty dollars, as I didn't finish the week. Now that I think of it, I should have told him to shove the sixty, but I needed the money. Rose was counting on that extra forty dollars. Sorry, Rose. Will I ever learn?

* * *

I had a friend the other day tell me his eleven-year-old daughter came home from a soccer game. The daughter and mother were quite proud that she had a trophy, so the dad said, "Way to go, Wendy. What was the score when you won the game?" The girl said "Oh Dad, we don't keep score in the games. We didn't win; we lost. But isn't the trophy great?"

The guy told me he was dumbfounded. He didn't know what to say. Don't keep score and you get a trophy for losing the game? He said to me, "Believe it or not, she got the trophy for competing." He works in a highly competitive business where, if you are not successful, you are gone. In other words, no reward for second place. So the business of being rewarded for losing just blew his mind.

I got to thinking, isn't that the way Canada is going: "Don't worry about working hard and saving money. We will take care of you from the cradle to the grave."

What does that attitude of just compete, don't sweat it if you win or lose . . . what does that teach the kid for later on in life? If the work or the study gets too hard, float along, don't worry about it. What kind of outlook is that for life? What character does that teach the kids? You have to know how to win and want to win, and if you lose, dust yourself off and start all over again, like the song says. My brother and I were taught that old poem, "Don't Quit." Here is part of it:

When things go wrong, as they sometimes will
And the road you're trudging seems all uphill,
When the funds are low and the debts are high,
And you want to smile but you have to sigh,
When care is pressing you down a bit,
Rest if you must, but don't you quit . . .
Success is failure turned inside out . . .
So stick to the fight when you're hardest hit.
It's when things seem worst that you must not quit!

The school thinks they're doing the girl a favour, not humiliating her or hurting her confidence. They are just preparing her for a big shock when she faces the real world. You must face the slings and arrows along with the bouquets to be successful. I should know. I have a lot of arrows in me.

* * *

Cindy, my daughter, and I were having one of our coffee chats one day and she asked me, "How would you describe yourself as a dog?" We are both in love with all dogs. I thought for a minute and I said, "Cindy, I am what you call a street-smart dog. Let me explain how a street-smart dog compares to a normal dog. For instance, I have normal dogs—nice, well-behaved—but if they got out on their own in the streets, they'd be done. They would not know how to survive. But your dog, Lucy, Cindy, is street-smart. Put her on the street, she'd survive anywhere."

How'd she get like that? I'll tell you how. Lucy is a rescue dog. She has been kicked around, abused, lived in four different homes. The final home was pitiful. The people who had her moved from their apartment and just left her to die. No food, no water. She barked for help till her vocal chords went. Finally someone reported her and she was rescued. That's when Cindy got her. Lucy had the same personality as the dogs in Sochi, Russia. They survived on the streets somehow. They knew the score, knew when to run and knew when to stand, knew how to avoid cars. It was you either knew how to survive or you were gone. They knew how cruel people could be and by hook or by crook, they survived. (Till the Russians shot them.)

Cindy said, "And you consider yourself one of these dogs? I thought Grandma and Grandad treated you well."

Don: "Cindy I led a beautified life. My mom and dad gave me everything I wanted. I went to the Barrie Flyers. We won the Memorial Cup. I turned pro in Boston, bought a new car at twenty-one. Life was, as they say, a bowl of cherries. I married the love of my life, Rose, and we had a beautiful daughter. Couldn't have asked for anything more. I was like my dogs at home: happy not knowing the world, not prepared for the hard knocks. It all changed when, at twenty-three, Boston gave up on me. They were furious with me for playing baseball and hurting my shoulder after they asked me not to. In those days when you got in the bad books, you were history. There were only six teams to play for. They could do anything they wanted with your life. Hey, I deserved to be taught a lesson, but to send a kid of twenty-three to Eddie Shore, the devil's island of hockey, was really a kick in the teeth. But I was still enthused when I reported to Springfield. Happy and disappointed, but still ready to go—sort of like my dogs."

The very first day I had my heart broken and it was there that I knew I had to change to survive. Gone was my attitude of "Life is great, people are all good, good things happen to good people, etc." It became dog-eat-dog, survival of the fittest, and I learned, just like Lucy, that people can be mean just for the sake of being mean and you have to toughen up and get some savvy to survive.

Savvy, to me, is the most important thing in the world in my position to survive, you've gotta keep Kenny Rogers' hold 'em/fold 'em approach. Know when to fight and when to retreat to fight another day. The adage I like is "Sit in the weeds. Every dog will have its day." I know what you're thinking, folks, that's an awful outlook on life, but like Lucy, we had to think that way to survive. You don't last twenty years in the minors being a nice guy. The motto in the minors was "Do it to him before he does it to you." That's how I survived physically and mentally. That's how Lucy and I are still going. We survived in the jungle, there was nothing else you could do to hurt us. We had run the gamut of disappointment and getting kicked in the teeth.

I know, reader, you're thinking, "Boy, Don is really getting carried away with himself." Maybe you're right, but you never went through four years with Eddie Shore as his favourite whipping boy, riding buses for twenty years. Along the way I developed savvy. I knew somehow I would survive. There were a lot of bumps along the way. Many times I was fired, had no job. Nobody knows you when you're down and out. The saying is so true.

Like Lucy, I survived. In a way, people like Shore toughened me up. It's too bad we had to go through all that turmoil to get through life, but that's the luck of the draw, the way the cards are dealt. I'm not complaining about anything. Whatever I got, I deserved. I'm just telling Cindy I consider myself a street-smart dog. Lucy and I know the score.

* * *

The Lord works in mysterious ways. He's a wonder to behold. I gave myself a lot of credit about street smarts and survival, but it's funny how my life worked out when I was sent to Springfield.

For a long time, nothing seemed to work out right for me. Things went from bad to worse. As I look back now, things started to break up for me after ten years of tough sledding. Not only for me but for my family. It was a break and I didn't know it at the time. The Good Book says "God can do infinitely more than we can ask or imagine."

Back in the sixties after knocking around the American League, the Western and Central Leagues, and the Eastern Professional League, I somehow ended up Toronto Maple Leafs property. How, I still don't know. I reported to Leafs camp. I knew I was not going to make the cut and their farm teams were the Rochester Americans and the Denver Invaders. I had played in Spokane the year before in the

Western League and I liked the Western League, so I wanted to go to Denver and I told them so. Nope. Joe Crozier was the GM and coach. He wanted a tough guy and he said, "No way, it's Rochester."

I did my best to get out of Rochester, but Joe had his way. It so happened that Punch Imlach, who was GM and coach of the Leafs, owned a piece of Rochester and packed the team with young stars and veterans to win. We won three championships and one final in four years. The team went to Vancouver and I went with them. We won the Western League Championship. That's four championships in five years.

I retired and worked construction for two years until I got laid off. A friend, Bob Clarke, asked if I would coach a high school team. I didn't really want to, but did it for a friend. For two years I learned how to change lines, practice and win a championship from the other side of the bench. I still had no job and was desperate to make a comeback with the Rochester Americans at age thirty-six. I was named coach halfway through the season. (Rarely now does a player get made coach halfway through a season and is successful because he doesn't know how to coach.) Because I did Bob Clarke that favour, it was a piece of cake. We almost made the playoffs, but I got fired for being too close to the players, even though we had a winning record. No job again.

Got a call from Bob Clarke. He and some rich guys bought the Rochester Americans. They asked if I would like to coach. I said, "Yes, and I'll be GM." We got some great players nobody else wanted, made the playoffs, went to the league championship for the second year in a row and got beat out in the first round.

When I was feeling sorry for myself I got a call from my friend Harry Sinden, GM of the Bruins, asking me to go to Chicago. I had known Harry before. We played against each other, became friends. When they fired Bep Guidolin as coach, Harry asked me to coach the Bruins. If Rochester hadn't missed the playoffs, I would not have been asked to join the Bruins. I was successful with Boston: four first place finishes and the finals twice, and the semifinals. Got fired again for being too close to the players. Then I went to Colorado, a great bunch of guys, but no goalie in Hardy Åström. Fired for being too close to the players again.

That's when I was asked to do *Hockey Night in Canada*. The executive producer (the boss), Ralph Mellanby liked me and protected me and here I am, thirty-four years later, still on *Hockey Night in Canada*. As I look back on all of my firings and misfortune, I know the Lord was helping me through. I did not realize it at the time. God works in mysterious ways. He's a wonder to behold.

AFGHANISTAN

RON AND I HAD JUST FINISHED a game for *Hockey Night in Canada*. We had our usual after-game bucket of beer, six apiece, on ice. We started this routine when we travelled a lot in Canada. When we would go to the bar after a game it would end up a big party, so we decided the best way to keep it simple was to get the beer in the afternoon and put it on ice in Ron's room. Popcorn is Ron's favourite, and peanuts for me, and watch a ballgame or hockey game and discuss the world—sometimes heated, mostly fun times. "Munchies Time," we called it.

When things go wrong on the set of *Hockey Night in Canada*, and it happens a lot, when I would be in a tantrum, Ron would hold up six fingers, meaning six cold ones waiting in the room, and I would say, "You're right," and calm down.

These meetings, like I said, were usually fun, but sometimes they would get so heated I would leave the room ticked off, but in the morning we would meet. It would be awkward for a bit. After a while, we were back to normal.

Except one time. The situation was this: Ron and I would sit up in the top row of the arena during the morning skate or practice. At one time, Ron used to hang around down on the bench, close to the players, until I straightened him out. I told him that media who hang around the dressing room or bench are considered floaters by the players, so from that day on we sat at the top of the building.

So one day, this media guy comes up to the top to say hello and Ron says, "Tell us what happened on that goal." And the guy can hardly wait to tell us and let me know how smart he is and how dumb we are. I say to Ron, "You dumbhead, don't you ever ask a reporter or a guy on another TV station about a play we are supposed to know. We are the experts. Do you know what he is telling his colleagues? That he had to straighten out the *HNIC* guys—they didn't know that play." We go at it that night and we meet for breakfast. We get into the argument again; we go and go and we go so long that when we get to the buffet, it's closed.

He has learned to not talk about me to reporters.

I remember I said something about a Canadian player for Montreal on *HNIC* and it caused trouble. We were walking back from the Forum, and Ron said he helped me by saying to a reporter that I didn't mean what I said and was sorry I said it. I said, "Are you nuts? It will be thought that I feel bad about what I said [I didn't] and there will be a headline that I apologize." Sure enough, the next day's headline: CHERRY APOLOGIZES. But he has learned over the years that we are all fair game and we have to watch our backs, and I must admit I look forward to our sessions.

So Ron and I had just finished the game in Vancouver and we were into our third beer and I was feeling very uneasy. The reason was we had just done a tribute to one of our "fallen soldiers" in Afghanistan. The soldier looked about eighteen years old. I know I get letters from the moms and dads thanking me for paying tribute to their sons, and when we are in airports and we meet the soldiers just back from the war, they thank us for recognizing them. The ones that get me are the ones that are going back to Afghanistan and say they can hardly wait to get back to the war. When I ask, "Why would you want to go back to that place?" they always say, "We are a team and they are our buddies."

I know I get ripped by some for glorifying war and they say *HNIC* is for hockey, not for a political statement, but mostly the media goes along with it. I always have that uneasy feeling. I feel sometimes like a phony, but I am being thanked and these beautiful, brave guys and gals are getting killed. It all came to a climax, as they say, that night in the hotel with Ron. I made a decision there and then that I had to go to Afghanistan that year. If I'm going to talk the talk, then I have to walk the walk. I was going to go that year, and I was going to go at Christmas. Ron says, "Be careful, Grapes. Are you sure it's not the pops talking?" I say, "Could be, but the decision is made and I'm going. I have to go."

I'm lying in bed that night, thinking about my decision, and again I get that uneasy feeling. Am I being a hot dog for attention again? Am I going at Christmas to be a hero? Sometimes you can't win. There is no turning back now.

Luba says one day, "You know you are going to Afghanistan in two weeks."

"You're kidding me—in two weeks?" says I. I'm one of those dumb guys who makes a commitment and thinks the time is never coming.

I go to the doctor for a checkup, some shots, but first of all I take a combat jacket to my tailor to have it custom-fitted. Vanity, vanity, thy name is Don.

As the day approached, I'm thinking, "Am I really going to Afghanistan?" I know Ron was secretly going, too, but I found out later he couldn't go. His dad had become ill.

The day came to depart. As I drove to the airport with my wife, Luba, it was very quiet. She was not too happy with me flying to Afghanistan—I think, deep down but never said, that I was too old to fly to Afghanistan. Imagine!

As I look back now as I write this, I guess I was the oldest guy, but you must realize, I think I'm thirty-two years old. I've always thought that. Why thirty-two? I don't know. I must have been at my toughest.

As I'm checking my bags, it all seems unreal. An Air Canada rep meets me and says my party is in the Air Canada room. My party? I didn't know I had a party to go to! I go to the Air Canada room, and there I meet my party: Jimmy Mac, a goalie from Winnipeg and a Canadian and entertainer who never stops with the Rodney Dangerfield routine, and a French singer, Dany St-Arnaud.

Jimmy Mac goes into his Rodney act and says, "Hey Don, do you know that the troops in Afghanistan right now are the Van Doos? You won't have to worry about the Taliban. Watch out for the Van Doos."

The Van Doos are the Royal 22nd, the famous French regiment. I'm going to entertain guys who won't even know

what I'm saying. I say to Jimmy, "Jimmy, these guys won't
even know what I'm saying."

"That's okay, Don, nobody understands you in any
language."

We board the plane. Luckily, I'm beside Jimmy Mac, who
is an okay guy, and as I look out the window, I say to myself,
"How did I get myself into this?" and I think back to the
session with Ron when he asked, "Are you sure it's not the
pops talking?"

I wonder. It seemed like a good idea at the time.
Remember, time to "walk the walk." I made the decision—
no more negative thinking. I'm going, and I'm going to be
dynamite and I'm going to enjoy myself. I'm saying this, but
wondering, "Do I mean it?"

Jimmy Mac is so pumped and never shuts up. I can see
he likes to give people shots. He gives some to me. "Grapes,
I think it's great you're going to Afghanistan when the
French troops are there. It's like you're extending a friendly
hand between you and the French."

I can tell you what I answered, but it's physically impossible.

The French singer doesn't say much, but just smiles. I
know he's going to be the hit.

It seems we are flying forever, and I can look around and
everybody looks so comfortable in their casual wear. Why
do I have to be so vain that I must travel in a suit, shirt and
tie? Ron and I are the only ones in the media who travel in
suits and ties. Much to our regret, when the finals run into
late June and we're in the heat from places like L.A. and
Tampa, the shirt looks uncomfortable—and they are, but
you are who you are.

We finally land in Germany, and we are met by some reps and then take off for Doha, Qatar. We land and are driven to our hotel. Checking in, I am invited to the hotel bar by a soldier, retired General Laurie Hawn. Never one to turn down a request for a beer, I agree.

I must say it's a great bar—English music and all. Ten soldiers all around a big table. Well, the suds are flowing and they order chicken wings and ribs, piled high in grease. I never eat chicken wings, even though I used to go to the Anchor Bar in Buffalo with the Bruins. It was famous for inventing Buffalo wings. That's what they called them in the seventies. They were invented by a woman everybody called Maw.

After the game, the Bruins would plow into the wings, but I've never eaten greasy stuff, so I just drink beer. I'll never forget Maw bringing these wings to the players. They would eat there often. She loved the Bruins.

The wings at this hotel were extra greasy. I hadn't eaten all day, so I dove into the pile with two hands. We are having a grand time. Hey, this is pretty good so far. Everybody says good night. A good night was had by all.

Back to my room after a ton of greasy chicken wings. Why, oh why, did I eat so many of those greasy wings? And of course, the pops were flowing.

I woke up at 4 A.M. and my big toe is killing me and it's all red and swollen. I can hardly walk. I get back into bed and I can't stand the sheets touching my toe. I'm in agony. It feels like it's broken. I sit up all night with a can of cold pop on the toe. It does no good.

Big day ahead, such as it is. I get dressed and can hardly

put my shoe on. Down to the lobby where I'm asked why I'm limping. I say I stubbed my toe. They buy it. The plane can't go—mechanical difficulty. Better on the ground than in the air. They decide to go to a museum. Can't show weakness, so off we go. The museum is mostly some vases and stuff. They decide to go shopping. Got to go with them, can't be chicken. I limp along. I notice the natives never look you in the eye and walk head-down. These guys are supposed to be friendly, but you could almost feel that hate. Big shots walking around in our house was the attitude. My toe is throbbing.

I walk along with the soldiers, and they open up to me. We have some politicians along and they have nothin' but contempt for them. One soldier says a left-wing politician got headlines when they sent stuff to the people once, including saws. The soldier says, "You know what they do with them? They cut them into pieces and use them in the bombs that they have planted along the highway. Cover the saw and bomb with earth. The saw is a perfect cover for the bomb." The road to hell is paved with good intentions.

Finally, the bus comes to take us to the hotel. My toe is worse—no good. I am starting to think it's not a broken toe, but something worse. Can't sleep.

Now, I'm ashamed to tell you, it's gout. It can't be, I think. I've seen movies. It's the old lords, with feet up on a footstool, that get it. Everybody laughs at their pain. What happened? The gout came after eating all those greasy wings and beer. I find out later it's the worst combo for gout. When I get home, I looked up "gout" and the word "excruciating" comes up. I can believe that.

We are in the lobby the next morning, ready to go, but we're told to wait. While we are in the lobby, a sad thing happens. The owner of the hotel has put the most expensive golf cart in the world in the lobby. It has gold on it. So everybody takes turns sitting in the cart to get their picture taken. While I sit in the cart, this guy all sharped up comes in the lobby with this gorgeous woman. He is hurrying her to the elevator. She is a "woman of the night," as they say. As she passes me, she says to the guy, "Wait a minute." She speaks perfect English. She asks if it is all right to sit with me in the cart.

"Be my guest," says I. She sits beside me, and the guy she is with is fuming mad. She turns to me. I look into her eyes. They are the saddest eyes I have ever seen. They are full of pain. Looks like she's on drugs.

She asks me if she can kiss me. She gives me a peck on the cheek and is gone. I'll never forget the hurt and pain in those eyes. I look around, and everybody has been watching. One soldier hollers, "Hey Grapes, congratulations. You just kissed the United Nations!" Ah well, you can't win them all.

We get the news: no plane. To tell you the truth, I'm not too unhappy because I don't know if I can walk. Things start to happen when Peter MacKay, the minister of defence, arrives. We obtain a gigantic Hercules. It is so big it can handle about four tanks inside. We get in the plane. The ceiling has got to be forty feet high and thirty wide, little chairs along the side. The soldiers are great, give us boxed lunches, do everything to make us comfortable. We take off to the compound. You can't hear a thing, it's so loud inside.

We finally land, and a truck of soldiers meets us and away we go. One soldier, when asked if any of the Taliban ever attack, says they're around. "In fact," he says, "last week, they sent some rockets into the compound." I think he was just having some fun with us.

Jimmy Mac and I are being shown around. When we are shown the hockey rink where they play ball hockey, two soldiers from the stands holler "Hey" and come to see us and say hello. I say, "What part of Canada are you from?" They're U.S. soldiers from Rochester, New York. They were glad to see somebody from home.

We are shown a little building that has a bed and a shower for each of us. They're all right by me.

Peter, when I told him I would go to Afghanistan, he kept saying, "You'll be safe behind the wire."

I said, "Are you going outside the wire?"

Peter said yes.

I said, "Okay, then, let's go."

I must explain something here. We are going to try to cram three days of visits into one and visit five spots.

I try to sleep with my toe. Impossible because the sheets actually cause pain.

Next day, we are driven to the Chinook helicopters. Let me explain about the Chinook helicopter. It's the one you see in the commercials where it opens up at the back and the paratroopers jump out. They have two big machine guns at the front. This is getting severe. They give us combat jackets, helmets. Have to have my custom shirt and jacket underneath. Why the heavy jacket? I'm told it will be freezing tonight.

We land at the first post, tanks all around and artillery. We meet the Van Doos. The first thing I notice is how young they are and how fit they are. They remind me of hockey players, primed and ready to go for anything. We stand in a circle, and I have to admit, it is a little strained to start, but when Chief of Defence Staff General Walter Natynczyk shows up, he breaks the ice. We take pictures and sign autographs and everything is okay. We say our goodbyes and go on to the next post.

For some reason, I was alone on this visit, but at the next camp, Jimmy Mac and the French singer, Dany St-Arnaud, are with me. I do my best. Jimmy Mac is terrific, but Dany, the French guy, was the hit as expected. He sang French songs and they sang along. Oh well, I did my best. Goodbye again, into the helicopter again.

This is where we saw our first American group, and it was kind of sad. They were a forlorn lot. You could see their attitude was different than the Van Doos'. One of the American guys said to Jimmy Mac, "We've been here for nine months and we can hardly wait to get out." Who could blame them? They were a sullen group. I did my best again, but not very good. Jimmy Mac did good, but again Dany, the French singer, had them eating out of his hand, especially when he sang songs about home and America. They didn't know me and couldn't have cared less. Goodbye and on to the next post, where Peter MacKay and General Natynczyk serve Christmas dinner to the troops. Kind of sad to hear them singing carols from home.

The next post is the biggest, most spread out and has the

biggest artillery piece you have ever seen. Evidently, it can fire and hit miles away. They ask if I would fire the piece at the Taliban. I have to lay my jacket down to walk to the piece. My toe is killing me. I tell the soldier who is helping me, "Watch my jacket, please." I am not thrilled at this long walk, but this is what I'm here for. I reach the artillery piece, and it actually scares you, so I sign the shell—something like "Here's looking at you" or something stupid like that. I pull the cord. It is so loud, the ground shakes. On the way back, it's starting to get dark and I'm freezing. I get back—no jacket. Can't complain, can't be a sissy.

I got to mention Jimmy Mac here. I would not have been able to continue without Jimmy Mac. It was murder to continue to walk on the stones that were at the posts. They were rocks, not pebbles. Just big enough to make walking miserable. Once in a while, he could get a Jeep to give me a hand if we had a long way to go.

At one of the posts, it's a long way to go to the toilet, so Jimmy has a U.S. marine drive me. I say I would like to go to the washroom. He drives me along the route, and finally we come to a building that says "Showers." I figure there's a washroom in the building. I go in—no washroom. I come out and say, "Where are the toilets?"

He says, "You wanted to go to the washroom. This is where we wash. If you wanted a toilet, you should have asked for a toilet, sir."

He must have thought Canadians are strange people, having to go pee and asking for a washroom. Come to think of it, he's right, but Jimmy is always there to help me with my big toe, which he thinks is broken. I'm too embarrassed to tell him I have the gout. Jimmy and the French guy, Dany, are the hits again.

I told Peter if he was going outside the wire, so was I. We go outside the wire for sure when we go far out into the desert to visit the Canadian Special Operations Task Force. They are a secret operation that includes snipers. When the regular army needs a special force to go and straighten things out, no matter how bad the situation is, these are the guys. No mercy asked and no mercy shown.

The commandant gives us a lecture on the history of the very building we are going to. It was occupied by the Taliban, and they stay there as if to say, "Take us if you can." We are told to take no pictures and about the tight security. We walk into a room of about 150 people, and they start yelling my name—standing O. Dany and Jimmy Mac give it a try, but it's my time to shine. Jimmy and Dany have shone all day, but it's mine now. I answer questions, tell jokes. I'm getting a little punchy by now, but loving it. After the pictures start, I look at the commandant. He just shrugs as if to say, "Go ahead." They take so many pictures the camera overheats and has to rest to cool off. I was having my picture taken with some young guys and they said, "Grapes, we're the snipers." I have to tell you, folks, I started to tear up just being around those guys.

I'm asked if I would drop the ball at a ball hockey championship game. They have waited till we came for the game. We watch the game from the roof, looking into the courtyard below. It's a barn burner of a game. They're playing for keeps. The building is built like a fort. I ask a young soldier about the Taliban and he says, "Don, see that ridge over there about two or three miles? The Taliban are just over there." He sees the look on my face. He says, "Don't worry, they won't bother us." Evidently, when the special forces go out at night, they don't go looking for prisoners.

I tell you, it's a strange feeling to stand on the top of a building with a beautiful moon shining down, watching a ball hockey game, knowing the Taliban are just over the ridge. As I gaze at the full moon and look around at these proud, brave, utterly fearless warriors, I feel proud to be Canadian. I wish every Canadian could experience that feeling. I will never forget that night.

(The special forces later sent me a framed picture of them with their special knife and a plaque that says, "From Warriors to a warrior. Thanks for your support." It is in a place of honour in our house. I asked if I could show it on TV. They said don't even mention it.)

I suddenly grow sad as I look around at the young soldiers, knowing that some of them won't come back, and I thank the Lord for the opportunity of meeting them. All good things must come to an end, and it is an emotional parting. It is very silent on the drive back to the helicopter. We all have our own thoughts.

Back in the giant helicopter, freezing, no windows and with no warm jacket and my thin dress shirt, I'm just asking for it. The guys on the machine guns open up. I ask the soldier next to me, "What gives?" He says the helicopter in front of us had gunshots fired at it, so these guys are firing to keep the Taliban heads down.

I have to tell you that, about this time, with five visits in one day, my toe, the cold, I really didn't care what happened.

I tell ya, I'm looking forward to some sleep, but I learn if we hurry we can catch a plane to Kabul and be on our way home. Back to the little room, quick showers, still dripping wet, packing fast, throwing things in my bag to catch that plane. A knock on the door. The woman driver. "Need help?" Now I'm starting to get irritated. Run to the van, get in and sit.

Don: "What's going on? I thought you said we had to hurry to catch the plane?"

Soldier: "We have to wait."

Don: "Whaddaya mean we have to wait? What for?"

Soldier: "The French guy to blow-dry his hair."

We miss the plane by ten minutes and have to sit in the airport all night to catch the one in the morning.

We have another marathon trip back. Jimmy Mac is still doing Rodney somehow. I've lost my beautiful Canadian cufflinks. We land in Washington in the middle of a snow-storm. Planes are delayed to be de-iced. We line up for tickets, we line up for customs. Imagine flying from Afghanistan to the States and we line up for security; all the while, flights are being cancelled. We get on the plane. Half-hour delay being de-iced. We land, say goodbye to good guy Jimmy Mac, limo home. My toe's gout has moved up to my ankle. Haven't slept in thirty hours. Outside the door, Luba has a little umbrella taped to a can of beer and a sign that says WELCOME HOME. She's walking through the door and asks, "How was it?"

Piece of cake!

* * *

Now, my buddy Jimmy Mac wanted to get his two cents in and tell you about our trip, too. Here's his version of the story:

A funny thing happened on the way to . . . Afghanistan? What did I just get myself into? I had been doing standup comedy for over twenty years at this point and just finished eight years of live television when I received a call from my agent in Toronto. "Hey Jimmy Mac, how's it going?" To which I replied something along the lines of, "Okay. Why, what's up?"

The conversation went on about a booking around Christmas 2010, and that if I was tired of the cold Winnipeg winter and wanted the promise of warmer weather, along with a mountain view and sand surrounding me, then "Have I got a gig for you!" I mean, honestly, who in their right mind would want to go into a war zone and perform for the Canadian troops when they could be safe at home with family over Christmas? A "true Canadian," that's who!

I am too old to be in the military, and my hockey days are long past, so the only way to be on the "Team Canada" roster at this point and do something for the country I love—and the men and women who sacrifice their lives for my right to say no to this trip—was to accept the offer. So I did! I didn't even hesitate; I said, "Book it!" I still remember that day: my body was buzzing because I'd just accepted a showbiz gig like my comedic heroes of the past—Abbott and Costello, Bob Hope and many others who actually performed for the troops. However, if you know me, only one thing scared me more than the war: *I hate to fly!* I also had to break this news to my family in a way that made them understand why I wouldn't be available for Christmas dinner.

How do you break such news? It went basically like this: "So I have a gig this Christmas, and I will be performing for the troops . . . in Afghanistan. Now, before anyone decides to say anything, this is the end of the discussion. I am going. It is something I need to do for my country, and I can't think of the location being Afghanistan or what *might* happen to me over there in a war zone."

Now, the government was pretty tight-lipped on the details of the trip and who was going to be on the Team Canada roster, though I did manage to get one name that had just been confirmed: Don Cherry.

So let me get this right. I am a Canadian male, grew up playing hockey (still play), and live for Saturday night's *Hockey Night in Canada* where *nobody* is allowed to speak during "Coach's Corner." And hockey icon Don Cherry is on the trip? Well, thank you, Canada, for the Christmas gift of a lifetime! I get to perform on the same bill as one of my hockey idols!

I have to say that, working on television, I've interviewed many famous people along the way, and the only time I was ever nervous around a guest was interviewing Ken Dryden, who was my hero as a kid and the reason I became a goalie. I only had thirty minutes with Dryden, but soon I would share seven days with Don Cherry!

I have never kept a diary of a trip before, but this was different! This was going to be a trip I did not want to forget, and that's why I can recollect for you my rendition of this adventure.

I was sitting in the airport VIP lounge, waiting for the rest of Team Canada and our departure to Germany, Doha and eventually Kandahar, when all of a sudden I saw a figure appear in a doorway, dressed to the nines in a black overcoat. There he was, my hockey idol and tell-it-like-it-is guy, *Don Cherry!* Remember those nerves I said I had when I met Ken Dryden? Double it! We all were introduced to everyone, and Don was friendly to everyone and signed whatever we had with us, and then we were all whisked away to a private area for a briefing on the trip. Don started telling a few stories and then turned his attention to me as I was sitting across from him. "Look at those tattoos!" he said. Long story short, I have a hockey sleeve of tattoos, which includes Dryden's masks, Peter Puck and one particular tattoo that was hidden from view on my bicep: a tribute to Don Cherry. It is a maple leaf, with a high collar and black-and-yellow checked tie (the Bruins' colours).

We took a few pictures, and I posted mine on Facebook. During our prep, as the officer was explaining the trip agenda, I piped up and asked why we were not now making it into Kabul? Before the officer could answer, Don hit me in the arm and yelled, "Don't argue!" in a voice he uses on Ron MacLean on a regular basis. We had a good laugh about it. This yell was to become a regular occurrence over the next few days, and become the cornerstone of a friendship that continues to this day. I will explain later, but for now, off to Germany.

A few plane issues caused delays before the next fifteen-hour flight into Doha, Qatar, but that was no big deal. My seat mate (lucky me) was Don. We talked hockey, he gave me some coaching tips, and since I also coach goalies, he gave me a few helpful drills he always used. And we talked some comedy. It was the regular talk a celebrity would have with a regular Average Joe like me, but that was about to change.

He nudged me after a few minutes of quiet and said, "I don't know why we're here. You know we are performing for the French troops! You're from Winnipeg, out west, and I get in trouble with Quebec all the time! What if they don't like me?" Now he was being serious. He loves our troops and was sincere in his hopes the guys would like him. There was no ill meaning in his concern; he just really wanted the Canadian kids to be happy he was the one visiting.

It was amazing to get to know Don Cherry off-camera, away from the spotlight for a while, where—believe it or not—he has a sensitive side. He may kill me for telling you that!

Once we landed in Doha, we were met by Canadian military personnel and taken to our hotel. First thing on the agenda after checking in was a beer with Don and the rest of our Canadian crew. Did I say beer? Just one? Let it be known I prefer to have a rum; however, when you don't order the first round, you get what is delivered to the table. War stories, hockey stories and jokes—and now into pint number four. Wrap up the night and head back to the hotel. This was when Don noticed I hadn't finished my beverage! Any opportunity to yell at me, he took. "What are you doing? Finish that! Never leave one behind. You're Canadian and from Winnipeg! What would your dad say?" Beer four downed. Headache to follow.

The next day in Doha is where Don learned we were more similar than he realized. Neither of us liked the museum the group was taken to, and when a political question came up regarding Quebec separation, I spoke my mind, which also seems to get me in some trouble—much like a certain "Coach's Corner" star! Of course, this added to our growing friendship. Upon leaving the museum (thank God), Don delighted us with a few more stories, which included one about how watching "Coach's Corner" actually saved a life.

During an ice storm, a member of an NHL player's family was about to go outside on their farm and check on the livestock. Upon hearing the theme music to "Coach's Corner," he decided to watch Don instead, and at that particular time, the barn collapsed. Because the farmer stayed in the house, no one was killed. A few chuckles followed the story, and I decided to add my two cents: "There you have it, folks, right from the horse's mouth: watching 'Coach's Corner' can save your life, and that's no bull!" Big laugh, and Don loved it. He said, "You're just like MacLean! We should do a routine together out here with the troops, a team act."

That is where our rendition of "Kandahar Corner" began, and we wrote up a short script for the troops. It wasn't an Oscar winner by any means, judging from the actual notes I still have, but it was perfect for two hockey-crazy entertainers that were not in a rendition of *Bullets Over Broadway*, but more like *Bullets Over Afghanistan*. An example would be something like me starting the act with: "Hey Don, what are the Canadiens' chances of winning the Stanley Cup this season?" Don would go into his thoughts and expert opinions and I would end it with something like, "So the Habs have a chance if the Price is right." This went on for six or seven questions that led to different stories and lasted about ten to fifteen minutes, followed by autographs and pictures with the troops.

It was later, at the hotel, that I started to notice two things about Don. He was starting to cough and lose his voice and he was limping. We had all been walking all day, so it was understandable—maybe a blister, or maybe he was just tired. We all made off to our rooms for a few hours of sleep before we were to meet at 10 A.M. in the hotel lobby and head to Kandahar Air Field (KAF). Don was still limping the next morning, so I asked him if he was okay and he told me he hurt his big toe before our trip. Typical tough guy, he shrugged it off and asked me to email his family and let them know we were doing just fine. I have seen this stubborn act, as many of us probably have with our own fathers. He took a few Cold-FX capsules and said he would be fine. No need for a doctor!

The trip thus far had been a thrill, to say the least, with the laughs and the tourists we were trying to be, but the fact you could be in some type of danger doesn't really hit you until someone from the military sits you down, hands you a consent form that absolves them of liability for any injury you might incur during your trip, and asks for your blood type—"just in case!" There is a reason your extended health plan doesn't cover certain destinations, and believe it or not, Kandahar is one of them!

(To this day, while crossing the border into the USA,

there are always odd looks and questions about why I have an Afghanistan visa and stamp in my passport.)

I took a deep breath, signed the release forms and we boarded the C-17 and headed for Kandahar. There are no beverage services on that flight, I'll tell you! The plane was a giant tin can with an engine and enough room to throw a football around—which we did.

We had two hours before our first show. I followed the three-minute shower rule (in a war zone, you've got to save water) and get ready for "Kandahar Corner." The troops loved the routine and Don signed autographs for at least an hour afterwards. I noticed the limping again, but this time I didn't say anything to Don; I called over an officer and asked for someone to take a look at him. I have been around enough celebrities in twenty years to know when someone is getting tired. I had them get him water and into a theatre where he could sit and finish the autograph session. I asked if they could wrap it up soon so he could get the medic to look at his foot. A small break in the action left me alone with Don for a minute, and when I asked him if he was ready to head back to the barracks, he replied, "As long as everyone has come through here first." Don was as tough as nails, just as he portrays, and he'd do anything for the Canadian troops.

Finally, on our way back to our lodging, he gave me the usual nudge and said, "Great job tonight. We killed 'em tonight, Jimmy-Boy!" I became Jimmy-Boy, a nickname he gives to the players—the ones I have watched on television for years—that he respects. When someone gives you a nickname in a dressing room, it's a form of acceptance, and when your idol gives you a nickname instead of just calling your given name, well, that is a gift. For some reason, I snapped into my Rodney Dangerfield impression: "Are you kidding me? No respect at all! I was kidnapped by the Taliban and the military said keep him!" Don had a great laugh with that, and whenever I noticed he was getting a little rundown or tired through the rest of the trip, I would throw a few Dangerfield lines at him, which always got a laugh and seemed to energize him. I enjoyed the fact that I could get a rise out of him when we all were in a war zone with the reality of an attack always near the back of our thoughts.

We headed back to Don's room, where we enjoyed a few "near beers" and some snacks that his wife, Luba, had packed for the trip, finished a cheese pizza from the mess hall and joked about the "warning siren" in case of a bomb threat. The military gives you instructions on the procedure to follow if there is a missile attack, but in true Cherry fashion, he said, "If you hear it, just duck!" A knock at the door, and the military medic was there now to look at his foot. I left for my own room, knowing he was finally getting attended to and that the limping would soon be addressed. We had a big Christmas day ahead of us, visiting five Forward Operating Bases (FOB) throughout Afghanistan, and I needed my new comedy partner in tip-top shape!

No sleep—awake all night, listening to the sounds of planes, helicopters and the odd sound of what might have been gunfire. Then it was 6 A.M. and we had a busy day ahead of us, visiting the troops. It's no use showering because your skin always feels like it's covered in baby powder. The soldiers call it "moon dust," and it looks like fog when it's in the air, but it's a fine dust you constantly inhale and hack out. Your teeth feel like they're covered in sand, and five minutes after a shower, you're dirty again. We throw on body armour, helmets and ballistic glasses. Felt like about fifty pounds, but all of it was necessary in case a missile hit our Chinook helicopter. Yeah, that's what they told us, and this was when it finally set in that we were heading outside the "wire" and into enemy territory.

Don was in prime form, yelling at me already. This time, it was about the seat belt in the helicopter that I hadn't buckled up. "Put it on!" he said. "What difference would it make if we were hit?" I argued. He barked back, "Don't be stupid. Just put it on!" So I did. Now, when I say Don yelled at me, it wasn't with a malicious intent. It was a form of affection, the kind you find in dressing-room talk or if you have ever watched an Abbott and Costello routine (especially the coffee shop skit). It was more in the style of a straight man, or the way he gets with Ron MacLean. Ours was a comedy act that was becoming quite entertaining to the troops who were travelling with us to the bases.

One officer asked me, "How long have you two known each other? Because it seems like you've been friends for twenty years." That was a huge compliment, as this was only day four of a journey never to be forgotten. We landed at our first FOB, and it was a football field-length walk to where the troops were waiting. Not a normal football field, but one with an uneven surface of rocks and sand. Not great for a healthy person, let alone someone with a broken toe, who might be the celebrity on the trip, but was also someone—nobody seemed to realize—not in his twenties, either!

Don is in remarkable shape, but add those extra fifty pounds of body armour, a busted toe and a cold on top of it, and I don't care who you are, this would be exhausting for anyone! At one point, away from the rest of the group, Don referred to his cold as "sucking swamp water." I have never sucked swamp water, but you get a good visual of how this might be difficult.

After the second FOB, I asked the first officer we met at the landing of base #3 if there was any way they could give Don a lift into the stage area where we were to perform. I told him the rest of us could walk these distances, but we needed to make sure Don got to and from the helicopter the same way. Don had no idea I had requested this for him. When the Gator utility vehicle the soldier was driving dropped him off, he turned to me and said, "See that, Jimmy-Boy? They got me a Kandahar Limo!" To which I barked back, in my Dangerfield voice, "Yeah, I ordered it for you. Now show me a little respect." Once again, not to be outdone, he yelled, "Well, that's the first thing you've done right this trip. Now get on the stage!" More laughs from around the group and we went into our "Kandahar Corner" routine. After the usual autograph session, we were invited for Christmas dinner with the troops. We actually served dinner for the troops, and after we were finished, Don grabbed a plate (picture Abbott and Costello again):

"Wanna eat?"
Me: No.
Don: Let's eat!
Me: No, I'm not hungry.

Don: Get a plate!

Me: I don't want anything!

Don: You're hungry, now get a plate!

Me: No, really.

Don: Get a meat pie and sit down!

Me: But I don't—

Don: Sit down and eat it!

At this point, the person serving was so confused and so busy laughing that he put the meat pie on my plate and we sat down. After I finished my dinner, Don looked at me and said, "I told you you were hungry!" We both had a laugh.

Time to get back to the Gator, get suited up in armour and off to base #4. This particular show was for both the Canadian and U.S. troops. Don said at one point before the show that he worried the American guys wouldn't necessarily recognize him and I would have to bail us out with comedy just in case. No problem, I thought. But he was about to turn that into a twist I wasn't expecting. He loved trying to get me into a situation—a prank of some kind for us to laugh about later. Our comedy routine together wasn't going as well as expected with the U.S. troops (Canadians loved it), so in mid-story he turned to me and yelled, "Give them some Rodney [Dangerfield], will ya! Do something here!" So I did a few lines and went back to the script. He stopped me and said, "Keep going!" So I did, and eventually told him so go sit down as I continued for another twenty minutes of my own standup act. Don later laughed about how he duped me into taking over and then thanked me for bailing the "team" out.

One more FOB to visit, and at this point we were all feeling the day catching up to us. This was a visit to the "special" guys, and I'm not even sure I am allowed to write about them, but let's just say they stayed in a base that was named after the home where Elvis Presley lived. Hope that hint is enough for anyone reading this. This was our last show on the tour, and by far the best of the bunch. I was asked if I could do Don Cherry's intro for him, and of course I said sure. What I didn't know was the officer introducing *me* had read my bio online and knew I did a Don Cherry impression! He asked me to introduce Don as only Don would introduce himself. Great—now I had to make sure this was a good one, and my voice had better be right on, or for sure I would get verbally berated by the *real* person I was trying to impersonate! "I tell ya, this next guest here, he's a tough guy, not afraid of the Taliban, no visor out here in the sandbox, and great guy and teammate . . . Don Cherry!" And with a big round of applause from the troops and Don laughing, he says, "Pretty good there, Jimmy-Boy. If I lose my voice here, you can take over." "Pretty good" in Don Cherry's vocabulary is the gold star on the school paper you aren't sure of before the teacher marks the exam. We finished this show, and those guys and girls loved him. I think it was the best one of the trip, at least for Don, as they couldn't get enough of his stories.

After the show, Don was again into the autograph session. By this point in the trip, everyone who had questions or concerns about Don was directed to me. I made sure he had his water and was somewhere he could sit down while taking pictures and chatting with each and every individual, so he didn't have to stand with the foot that was visibly paining him by now. Finally done, one last helicopter ride back to KAF and a sigh of relief that we made it back without incident.

Once again, I made sure Don got some medical attention and had to make sure he iced his foot every hour. By the end of this Christmas day, he said to me, "I don't know if I would have made it if it wasn't for you making sure I was okay, Jimmy-Boy. Thanks." I heard later from defence minister Peter MacKay that Don said, "He is the kind of guy I'd go to war with any day. That's a true Canadian right there."

In reality, looking back over that trip, at the beginning he was Don Cherry the celebrity, the *Hockey Night in Canada* icon I had watched for years. But at some point during the trip, he became my teammate, a teammate who was hurt, and if you watch any athlete when hurt, other teammates will help them off the field or the ice to get him to safety.

Going back to his earlier warning to "never leave one behind," it rings true. It was actually meant in the sense of finishing a beer, but it took on a more important meaning as a lesson about being a teammate: stick up for your players when they wear the same crest—or, in this case, the Canadian flag. So I didn't leave one behind. Now let me say this: even though Don had an injury, he was still the "hockey player" in the situation. He was just like his beloved tough guys and grinders he praises on television every week. At seventy-six years of age, with a busted toe, a cold that felt like "sucking swamp water," posing for over three thousand pictures and signing autographs in one day and walking over rocks and sand for over ten hours, not once did he ever complain or act tired or indifferent to any of the soldiers. He loved them all and made sure everyone was happy.

We had our own shorthand by the end, where I knew when to make sure he took a five-minute break from signing or taking pictures, but he always continued until the last piece of paper was signed or photo snapped. A Canadian hero to anyone who met him on that visit.

Our adventure wasn't quite over, as we still had to get home. I made sure everything was done for us, from checking our luggage to making sure he iced his foot before our flights. We boarded the plane for our long flight to Washington and chatted until the plane was safely in the air. And then he turned to me and said, "Well, we made it, Jimmy-Boy." And before I could respond, he hit me in the arm, said, "Now let's get some rest, so shut up!" and laughed as he reclined his seat.

I am not sure how many hours passed in what I believe was the deepest sleep I have ever had, but we awoke in Washington. We were guided to where our luggage was to be identified and I picked up mine right away. I noticed Don was chatting with the customer service person and trying to explain he didn't have his luggage claim tags. Why? Well, because I checked us in and didn't give them to him. So, trying to continue our string of one-upping each other, I wandered over to listen to their verbal exchange. I guess I could've stepped in to help, but I was having too much fun listening to the ordeal.

Finally, I said, "Why can't you get your bags?"

He looked at me and said, "You booked it, Jimmy-Boy! Where's our tags?"

"You didn't ask me for them!" I yelled, and we were all laughing at this point because I'd finally got him back at his own game.

Later, he told me of a story about travelling with Ron MacLean, and how he took Ron's passport out of his pocket. All good hockey-style pranks. Soon, we landed in Toronto, and the Christmas of a lifetime was about to end. We exchanged addresses and phone numbers and he said I could use him as a reference for any media or sports job I was going to apply for. That's an offer I have never taken him up on, although if the right sports position were to cross my path, I would be sure to call in that favour. He gave me the signatures he had promised earlier in the trip for the final piece of the tattoo on my arm. I hadn't asked him again since the first day of the trip; he just remembered and kept his word.

As we made our way to the exit, he stopped and said, "Where's your phone?" I took it out of my jacket, and he said, "Call your mother and tell her we made it." And so I did, and when she got on the phone, he decided to take the opportunity to let her know that "Mom and Dad raised a good kid." He handed me my phone, shook my hand and said, "You were the best part of the trip, and I don't think I would have made it without you there."

As he walked away, he turned for one last thought, and said, "Remember: don't argue with your mother, Jimmy-Boy. Keep in touch."

I watched him walk away and remembered something he had told me earlier in the trip, about how he doesn't like emotional goodbyes. What guy does? He never looked back, just stopped and signed an autograph for a kid who recognized him.

I'm not sure if I'll ever get a chance to go back to a military zone to perform again, and I know that I could not do what those brave men and women who join the military do for us. But I do know one thing: if, at some point during that trip, we came under some sort of fire or emergency, I would have taken a bullet for Don and would never have left that man behind.

SOCHI 2014

FEBRUARY 1, 2014. *Hockey Night in Canada*, Saturday night. I am meeting with Chris Irwin, head of the Sochi Russian Olympics. I am going to pitch to Chris and Trevor Pilling, head of CBC Sports. The pitch is I would rather stay here in Canada and do the games here the same way I did when the games were in Turin, Italy, where Brian Williams and I sat at a desk in Toronto and watched the games. It was a piece of cake. I fail in my attempt, and I hear through the grapevine that the reason is that Budweiser had sponsored my appearance.

February 4, 2014. My son, Tim, drives me to airport. I meet Mark Lee, an announcer from women's hockey. We check in—he says he knows where to go. We go to the lady at the gate, who sends us to another gate. We go to another gate, wrong gate. We are sent on a wild goose chase to different gates by people we can hardly understand. Finally, a good old boy recognizes me and takes me to the original gate: seven gates, fifteen pictures taken, twenty autographs. I'm in a cold sweat. We're back at the original gate Mark and I went to. Look, I realize everybody has to work, but do you not think it would be better for everybody if the people at Pearson Airport had command of the English language and had an interest in helping you? This is very frustrating.

I remember when I was with the Bruins, one of our players, as we entered Toronto was asked at the border, "How long have you been out of Canada?" and he answered (ticked off at the attitude), "Longer than you've been in it." Oh boy, did we do some scrambling with that one with the Mounties, but like I said, it is frustrating to be treated like a foreigner in your own country. There, I got that off my chest.

February 5, 2014. Eight hours over to Frankfurt, land, get our bags. Four elevators to get to our train to take us to another airport, four more elevators to get to our gate. We have seven hours to kill before our next flight, to Russia. The German customs guy looks at the passport, doesn't even look at me, is talking to another guy and tosses the passport back to me. Very rude, but who cares? We sit for six hours and then line up at the gate. Finally get to the gate. The lady says overweight luggage (it was okay in Canada) costs forty euros. Try to pay with Visa—no. Canadian money—no. U.S. money—no. Only euros. Where the hell can I get euros? Borrow some from CBC people, pay them in Canadian. It is a scam. Everybody gets scammed on the flight, and I hear the Australians got taken for $2,000. Cassie Campbell with *HNIC* got zonked for $1,800. Welcome to Europe.

Got about another four hours to Sochi. Land, first person I meet is a young Russian solider, looks like a hockey player. Clean and speaks perfect Engish. Hello, welcome. Very friendly. What a difference from Toronto and Germany. The customs lady smiles and says, "Welcome, have a good day." Perfect English. Can't believe we are in Russia. The people are friendly and polite and helpful, and speak English perfect, whereas in my country, Canada, at the airport, I can hardly understand anybody and they couldn't care whether you lived or died. I think I'm going to enjoy myself in Russia.

Kathy Broderick, the producer of the games, is there. She's got everybody arranged, van to the hotel. I check in. Ron MacLean is there with some beers and munchies. He takes a picture to send to Joe Warmington of the *Toronto Sun*. He has a front-page story about my eightieth birthday in Russia. Ron was just there to greet me. He has to go back to work all night.

February 6, 2014. Met by Warren Lowe from Edmonton, who is going to be my guide through this caper. I tell him we got to get some beer and munchies. He says we got to go to downtown Adler, not Sochi. We go downtown—I'm amazed it feels just like Mississauga. Somehow, I thought it would be different. Nice shopping malls. We get our beer. Only one Canadian beer or American beer: Budweiser. I get two two-fours. Back to the hotel. Opening ceremonies that night. I go to the lovely steamer they have in the hotel. As I come back to the room, the fireworks start. The window at the end of the hall has a window overlooking the fireworks.

I open the window and take my little Kodak I bought in a drugstore and take pictures. I wonder how they are going to turn out. (They didn't.)

February 8, 2014. Watch the women's team beat the Swiss 5–0. No contest. I even think the Canadians kept the score down. Leave at 2:30 A.M. for the Leafs–Hurricanes game for "Coach's Corner," finish the "Coach's Corner" and then, at the end of it, do an update of the women's game against the Swiss for that night. Finish it off at 6 A.M., back to the hotel and have three Buds at seven-thirty in the morning.

February 9, 2014. Day off. Radio and TV interviews. I look out my window and see a dog across the road. He is friendly to people; nobody pays attention. He is a stray. I remember reading where all strays were rounded up, and I hate to think what happened. I see another dog on my walk. I go and get some meat and bread and cut it up and go looking for him. Can't find him. Still up. I'm told that Christie Blatchford, columnist for the *Globe and Mail,* is upset too and is feeding them. Steve Simmons of the *Toronto Sun,* who is a good friend of Christie's, tells me she feeds them. It's true. Christie is known for no prisoners taken in her writing. Tough as nails. One time, I complained about something she had written about me and she told me to go and do something that's physically impossible. Great.

   She's concerned for the dogs, and I think my approach to life is a tough stance, like Christie.

   Both of us own English bull terriers. We are the only ones that seem upset about the dogs. I guess it is the old saying, "The tougher you are, the softer you are." And now Warren tells me somebody complained about the dogs and I haven't seen one since. Damn the insensitive people. I find out later that Ron has been feeding the dogs, too.

February 10, 2014. First time at the arena. Beautiful practice rink. All blue, watch Canadian women. We have a big team, whereas the U.S. has a small, quick team. There is no doubt who is going to be in the finals for the gold—Canada and the U.S.—but there is a doubt who is going to win. I have been to the rinks twice, have done at least eight interviews, mostly with the Russian press. Why do I do them? I have fun and it keeps me sharp. One asks me what I didn't expect in Russia. I say I'm surprised at how modern Russia has become. I went downtown to get some Buds in Adler, near Sochi, and the mall was just like in Mississauga. Very impressive. Reporter: "What did you expect?" "Well, to tell you the truth, we get the image of Moscow and women sweeping the streets."

Tim Wharnsby comes to me later and says, "Did you say this?" "Yep." "And did you say it's got rid of all the commies?" "No, I didn't say that, but it sounds like something I'd say."

Yesterday, I had two interview guys on at once: in front of me, a Czech reporter, and to my left, a Russian. The Czech was upset that I had given Tomas Hertl, the San Jose rookie, heck for hot-dogging a goal against Marty Biron. Hertl put the stick between the legs and it was a top-corner beauty, but the score was 6–0 for San Jose. I could not get it through the Czech's head that it wasn't the goal, it was the timing of the goal and the score. You don't humiliate goalies when you're up 6–o. If the game is tied, or winning by one goal, sure, but not at 6–o. He asked why I don't like Czechs, and I said I thought Hertl was a Russian. The Russian replied, laughing. I said I got nothing against Czechs, I liked Dominik Hasek and I admire Jaromir Jagr having a good year for New Jersey. Czech replied, "You didn't like his hair, you made fun." Yeah, I did. I was doing colour for Pittsburgh, and Mario and Jagr posed for the program, and I said it looked like Mario and his sister. When Jagr got hurt, they didn't know whether to send over his hairdresser, a jeweller or the trainer. Czech again: "You made fun of the way he celebrated a goal." Yeah, I never liked the salute after a goal. It pumped the other team up—when the other team beat Pittsburgh, the players gave the salute. And now do you see how he celebrates a goal? No salute, just a little fist pump. Nice, just like a Canadian.

The Czech sort of gave in on that one, but couldn't understand how Hertl's celebration was wrong. Look, I said, maybe in Europe you don't mind a guy acting like that. In fact, when I see European soccer, they do that stuff. But in the NHL, we don't do that. Czech: "You said somebody should hurt him." No, I didn't say somebody *should* hurt him; I said if he keeps acting that way, somebody *will* hurt him. (The kid got hurt three straight games and finally out for the year. Play with a bull, you get the horns.)

I know what you're thinking: "Why put yourself through all that with reporters you'll never see again?" It's a game, like I said. It keeps you sharp. Finally, I said to the Czech guy, "Do you know baseball?" Surprisingly, he did. He said by far Atlanta was his favourite team. I said I saw an Atlanta rookie last year hit a home run, stand and admire the home run, and then flip the bat. The first baseman gave it to him as he came to first base (also the first base coach) and the second baseman, the third baseman . . . and the catcher almost grabbed him. The manager of Atlanta got him in the corner of the dugout and had him against the wall, giving it to him. Now you could say, like you said about Hertl, just a young man excited about a goal. We don't do that here. Naturally, next time up, he got a ninety-mile-an-hour fastball in the ribs. The rookie never said a word, just laid his bat down and went to first. Never even looked at the pitcher. He knew it was coming.

There is a code we follow over here (in North America), the Czech said, and I seem to dictate it. No, I said, I just make sure everybody follows it.

All right, you know baseball, it's 7–0 Atlanta in the eighth inning, guy on first for Atlanta. He never, according to the code, tries to steal second. Finally, he agreed. Strange that he knew the code in baseball but not in hockey.

The Russian, meanwhile, came in with, "You don't like Ovechkin." I said, "Show me where I said I didn't like Ovechkin." No, again, what I said was I didn't like the way he acted after a goal, like clapping the glass after a goal or—the ultimate insult—when he scored the fifth goal in a row and laid his stick down and let it seem like it's burning. I said change or you're gonna get it, and he did.

How could I not like a guy who is leading the league in goals? I said to both of them after about twenty-five minutes, "Do you see the way Jagr acts after a goal now? No salute and the rest of the stuff, and you see how Ovechkin acts now after a goal, no clapping glass or burning stick. They act sensible now, like a good Canadian." I felt I had to straighten them out. They laughed and had their picture taken. My friend Warren Lowe from Edmonton—who is, as they say, taking care of me—said, "Boy, that was a long interview, and they gave it to you. Why do you subject yourself to that? Doesn't it wear you down?"

Nah, it's like a chess match: they try to get me and I get myself out of it. When they start a question, I'm answering it in my head as they say the question. I rarely get caught—and it's not like I'm clever or anything, it's just that I've done so many.

Warren: "What do you watch for in an interview?"

I can size a guy up pretty good. What you have to watch for is the guy in an interview near the end. What they do is get everything they want in a good interview, and now they go in for the kill. Some embarrassing question or a question to make you look bad. You see, they don't care if you stop the interview, because they already have a good interview, but they're hoping you'll get caught and say something to hurt yourself or storm out of the interview, and then you look bad and they've got a better interview.

Warren: "What do you do in that situation?"

I have a standard answer: "Hey, did you just get out of school? Think you can just get me on that one?" And I laugh. If he keeps it up, I just keep ridiculing him. I'm a master at it.

Warren: "Why do it, though? Isn't it draining?"

Nah, it's fun!

As you read this, Cherry thinks he's a clever fellow. Honestly, I come from the school of hard knocks. The only reason I get by with reporters is that way back I would get burned by them. So after a while, you get a sixth sense. I always have my guard up, and now, when I get into trouble, they take things out of context. Like that Russian reporter will take that one phrase, when he asked me about my view on Russia, all positive, except when I said I had the wrong impression of Russia as we see it on TV back home, women sweeping the streets. He'll put in that Cherry's impression of Russia is old women sweeping the streets, not that I'm impressed with Russia. But that's the name of the game. He's just doing his job, but as I get older and more experienced it's harder to catch me, and I haven't been caught in a while.

But back in the nineties, I let my guard down and got burned. It was with the Mississauga IceDogs, a new franchise in the OHL. To say we were having a tough time is an understatement. We were having a horrendous time, as Ron MacLean would say, and bad, too. Our first nine games on the road, we never scored, and we—or should I say, I—was no good. It was our third year, and the coach I hired, we just couldn't keep. We let him go and I kept my word, paid him $80,000. We couldn't afford another coach, so I had to coach. Talk about asking for it. But what could we do? We couldn't pay him and another coach, so I paid the price and did it. I was coaching and doing *HNIC* and my radio show five days a week. It was a tough go, and I was tired and no sleep.

The one paper had a female reporter who knew nothing about hockey. Her job was to get me, but she was so oblivious that she really never got me. But I must admit, she did her job. I remember one question: "The players say you don't keep your promises." It was true that I promised the players sweatsuits when we went on long bus trips. I was saving the suits to give them for Christmas presents. It wasn't all the players feeding her this stuff; it was one player. To describe him would be unfair, because he had many problems in life and still does.

I remember one young writer, he was just starting out in junior hockey—he was, as they say, a rookie and seemed a good kid—and just to prove I'm human, as I was caught up in all the turmoil, I let my guard down and was careless and I paid the price. The interview went well, we shook hands, and I said, "What a nice kid." The next day, I picked up the paper and was levelled by the kid. It was his chance, and I'm sure he got praised by his editor. I wasn't really furious at the kid, I was furious at myself, after all these years to get suckered in—no excuse. The kid was just doing his job to get ahead and I was the dumbhead, and I have to admit he never let up—there was no mercy, and we were an easy target. And it paid off for him: he rose up in the paper. That was sixteen years ago and he still gives it to me about the IceDogs. It's the way of the beast, though; he never mentions that the IceDogs won the Eastern Conference championship in year six. I was not there, but it was won with players we drafted high for finishing last (we had four first-overall picks in a row).

And while it might sound strange, it's good for me to take a shot now and then. It reminds me to be aware and to remember that the worse I look, the better the story for the reporter. So now, when I do an interview, I just think of this guy and how I got sucked in. As the song goes, "Won't get fooled again."

I must admit, not everybody is like this. For instance, the *Sun*'s Joe Warmington. I told him the week before Steven Stamkos made the decision to not go to the 2014 Olympics that Stamkos would not go. I told him, "That's between you and me," never doubting that he would scoop me. That's why people trust him, and again I don't doubt the kid, he was just doing his job and he did a good one.

But as I look back, the IceDogs were such an easy target. It was a bad idea from the start. When my friend Trevor Whiffen introduced me to an entrepreneur named Joel Albin with the idea to get a franchise in Mississauga, it sounded like a good idea. The mayor, "Hurricane" Hazel McCallion, was a hockey person. There were 600,000 people in Mississauga, and it had good minor hockey. But I pointed out we have no TV station, no radio, no daily paper in Mississauga. How were they going to know when we played?

The city, when we approached, said there'd be no arena till we got the franchise. The league said no franchise till we got the arena. To make a long story short, we ended up with the arena and the franchise, as it worked out, much to our regret. In the meantime, Brampton—right next door—got a franchise, too. As it worked out, two bad franchises, but here's the kicker that sealed our doom: Brampton had Scott Abbott, the millionaire who made his money on the game Trivial Pursuit, so they got their money two months before us. Because of this, they got all the first-round picks. It should have been they got a first round, then we got ours.

Instead, they got all the first-round picks, we got left in the dust. And to add to our misfortune, the arena was delayed and we played our first nine games on the road—not a prayer. And to add insult to injury, the refs' attitude was "Big stuff Cherry, we're not intimidated by him." And just to show that they were not, they piled on the penalties. Between all this, I took over the club. I was easy pickings, but I went in with eyes wide open and knew I would pay.

Boy, we were a failure at the gate and on the ice, but we took the blow, got our first-round kids out there. In fact, the last year I was there, more of our players got drafted by the NHL than any other Canadian Hockey League club, and only the London Knights were close to us. We had just started to turn the ship around. Unfortunately, I wasn't the captain that one of the owners wanted to see, and the deal was if one sold, all sold. The team went on to win the Eastern Conference championship in six years, but it made no difference. Just as predicted, no TV, no radio, no paper. They were still drawing flies.

The Lord works in mysterious ways; he's a wonder to behold. I didn't know it, or realize it at the time, but I was not cut out to be an owner or a GM. When we lost, I took it personally, and all this losing was affecting my health. I didn't realize it at the time, but people didn't want to be around me. Luba, my wife, stopped going to the games because she did not want to drive home with me after the games. So it was a blessing in disguise that we sold the IceDogs. The franchise moved to St. Catharines and is doing well.

That's me and my dad. Doesn't he look like he should be in *Boardwalk Empire?*

Mom and Dad are in the middle of the group. They're near Cedar Island in the Thousand Islands, Ontario.

St. Luke's Anglican Church. My teacher was Mrs. Bruce Hall. I apologize for acting up in Sunday school. I was a jerk. That's me in the back row, second from the right.

Me at sixteen with a broken ankle and my dog, Dudgeon.

After a Barrie Flyers practice when I was seventeen years old with my teammates Ross Hudson (left) and Billy Hope (right).

Me in a Leafs uniform, up for a cup of coffee.

In my Springfield
Indians uniform.

My Springfield Indian teammates (L to R): Cal Gardner, George
"Punch" Imlach (coach), Norm Johnson, Stan Bulik, me, Claude
Dufour, Floyd Smith, Bud Hillman and Tony Schneider.

Looking sharp behind the bench in the Boston Garden.

A tense moment against the New York Islanders. That's Ricky Smith, Davy Forbes, Danny Canney, me, Ron Grahame (L to R).

Taken somewhere in France. Sergeant Thomas V. Mackenzie, a relative, has the little white dog on his lap. He was a member of the 1st Brigade Canadian Field Artillery and was awarded a Military Medal and Bar. Sadly, he was killed four days before the end of the war.

Richard E. Palamountain, my grandfather, of the 4th Regiment Canadian Mounted Rifles. He fought at Vimy Ridge and was fortunate enough to survive the war.

February 11, 2014. Saw the Russians for the first time at practice. Look terrific. Big, fast. I was watching Russian TV; they had a made-for-TV program on the '72 series, and it was great. It showed where Bobby Clarke broke Valeri Kharlamov's ankle. Phil Esposito looked like a maniac. We looked like thugs. It ended where they won the first game 7–3, and didn't show when we won. I really feel the Russians are using that '72 series as a motivator. Listen to this: we have a young driver, a Russian. Nice kid, I like him. Warren asked him if he knew any Canadian hockey players. Right away, "Yes, Bobby Clarke," he answered. Not Crosby, not Gretzky, not Bobby Orr, only Bobby Clarke, who broke Kharlamov's ankle. I feel it's motivation.

The Russians look ready, eager. Saw us for the first time. Maybe it was the time difference or what, but we did not look as good as the Russians. But you don't win games in practice.

I did an interview with Jian Ghomeshi at the big studio of CBC here—good interview. He took me to task for not liking Europeans. I said it's not that I don't like Europeans, it's that I'm an extreme Canadian. Yes, I don't like Europeans in Canadian junior hockey leagues; they take a Canadian's spot. I feel for Canadian parents who spend thousands and thousands of dollars on hockey sticks, equipment and ice time, and then, when it's time for their kid to make junior hockey, teams parachute kids in from Russia whose parents never contributed one dime in Canada, never paid taxes. And let's be honest: if they pay for a kid to come all the way over from Russia and back again, and the Russian kid and the Canadian kid are equal in talent, who do you think they're going to keep? They have all that money invested— get real.

And did you know that they are bought suits and shirts and ties and extra clothing, and did you know that they get extra money, and did you know they and their agents dictate where they want to go and play junior in the Canadian Hockey League. For instance, when we were with the IceDogs, we were going to draft this certain player. His agent from Russia phoned and said, "Don't draft him, he is not coming to North America. He has got to go into the army." So we didn't draft him and he went to another team. We knew the agent was lying, but we had no choice. Yes, they have everything going for them, and our kids get the short end of the stick, and nobody says a word because if you do, you're considered a bigot.

I'm told on the QT that the Western League and the Ontario League want to stop the flow of Europeans, but the Quebec League won't allow it—for obvious reasons. They wouldn't be able to compete.

I say it, and I'll say it again, and I'll say it for your brother, your son or your grandson: the Americans are welcome in the CHL. They let our young men and women go to the States on college scholarships and help us. How do the Europeans help our kids? No, Canadian hockey leagues are for Canadian kids.

During the interview with CBC's Jian Ghomeshi, I tried to tell him I got nothing against Europeans. People think that when I say we're the best, it somehow puts foreign players down. I'm not saying they're bad; I'm saying we're good.

And some Canadians think that's a putdown to Europeans. I've never been able to figure that out.

Ghomeshi said I said that European players have no heart. I said I can't believe I said that. In fact, I never said it. After the interview, he came on the set and said I said it—he has it on video. I said, "When?" It was back in the nineties. Canada was behind 3–0 and we came back and won, and I was supposed to have said something about heart. I'll bet I said—and I'm going to find out—that we won because we had heart. In some circles, they would say that indicates that the Europeans didn't have heart. See what I mean?

This afternoon, I have to leave here at 3:00 P.M. and do the opening of the women's hockey, do "Coach's Corner" at the end of the first period, stay for the game and then do another "Coach's Corner" for the replay back to Canada. When I'm there, I'm going to see the producer of the Jian Ghomeshi show and run the part where I was supposed to have said Europeans have no heart. I'll bet I said we have heart; if I'm wrong, I'll put it in this part of the book. I'll end for now till I come back home after the game. It's 9:30 A.M. (I didn't bother Jian or his producer. I got too busy.)

February 12, 2014. Sochi, Russia. Everything here is in English and Russian. The signs on the buses, the songs for the figure skaters, the songs at the Games, in the hotels and at the airport. Do the Quebec language police know about this? It's ironic that the Russians have English to help us in Russia.

The women beat the U.S. today 3–2. Great game. Hayley Wickenheiser, a goal and an assist. Ron and I struggled

today, not in top form. The location was not good, still bothered by dogs.

February 13, 2014. Can't sleep. I don't think our "Coach's
Corner" shows have been very good. I've got to make a
comeback in the Canada–Norway game. Kathy and I agree
we have to get better clips. Lu phoned at 7:09 A.M. all upset.
Believe it or not, they showed a young giraffe in Denmark
getting its head cut off on TV.

I am still upset about the "Coach's Corner" We did when
the Canadian women beat the US 3–2. I just have to do
better. I come all this way and don't do a good job. I expect
to hit a home run every "Coach's Corner" and can't stand it
when I hit a single or strike out, which I feel I have been
doing. This gig is different. During the NHL season back in
Canada, I've got stuff to put on "Coach's Corner" from all
the games the week before. There's lots to choose from.
Here in Russia, I've got to have stuff from the games that
night. I'm not getting what I want and pull a tantrum. I'm
looking bad.

We do another "Coach's Corner" for the game back in
Canada at 7:00 P.M. that's shown there at 12:00 P.M. (confus-
ing, I know). After the game, Kathy Broderick and Warren
Darling . . .

(Don't you love that name, "Darling"? When I coached
the Boston Bruins we had a scout called Gary Darling. He
phoned one of our young prospects called Jimmy Petty—a
wild guy whose hair looked like seaweed, so we called him
"Seaweed." Well, our scout called Seaweed and said, "Hello,
I'm the head scout of the Boston Bruins, Gary Darling."

Seaweed did not believe him, thought someone was playing a joke, so he answered, "Hello, I'm Jimmy Sweetheart of the Rochester Americans.")

. . . Anyhow, Warren and Kathy and I walked over to the CBC building and did a live interview with Heather Hiscox. What a lovely woman.

After the interview, I go back to the hotel. Ron goes to the CBC building and works all night. I never see him. He works night and day and is getting a little testy, but who can blame him with that schedule. Our rooms are beside each other. When he is not on TV, he is in his room sleeping, with a "Do Not Disturb" sign on the door. I always close my door quietly.

I don't see the dogs around anymore. My room overlooks the whole compound. I see the complete picture: security gates, etc. I went looking for the dogs to feed them. I had some bread and meat, but I saw no dogs. It's a cruel world. I can't get over the country of Denmark allowing them to cut off the young giraffe's head. The Copenhagen Zoo had offers from other zoos to buy the giraffe, but they killed it and fed it to the lions and showed it on TV. Dogs gone, giraffe murdered, what a world we live in.

The same day I'm at the CBC building, I notice a guy with a picture of his dog on his leash. I say, "What a nice dog."

"Yeah," he says, "it's a hunting dog. We hunt together."

He shows me a picture of him and his dog standing over a beautiful big moose with enormous antlers that he had shot. What a gorgeous beast lying dead. I just don't get it. I know what you're thinking, "what a suck."

It's 4:30 P.M. This is one game that Ron and I are going over to together. He tells me he will knock on my door as he's worried I will be too early and disturb his sleep.

We do the game. Canada wins 3–1. No contest again. We outshoot Norway 14–2 in the second period. I come back to my room and watch the Russians beat Slovakia. Ron went to the CBC studio to work all day.

February 14, 2014. Up at 6:30 A.M. and went for a walk (looking for dogs again). As I am coming down the hall to my room, I see Ron going to his room. He has worked all night. This Olympics is turning in to a nightmare for him. Of course, he doesn't complain. If he did, he knows I would bug him, but to tell you the truth, he looks beat and tired.

I leave at 7:00 P.M. for the Canada–Austria game. Another cake walk. It was Canada 6, Austria 0.

February 15, 2014. Got to liven up "Coach's Corner." Warren and our trusty Russian driver, Rustelian (I call him Rusty) drive downtown to pick up some stupid-looking hats—one a lion, another a rabbit—for "Coach's Corner."

Watched the USA–Russia game. Russia lost to the U.S. in a shootout. The Russians got stiffed. They scored the winner when the game was tied 2–2, but the goal was called off because the net was off a little. Earlier in the game I had noticed that the pegs that hold the net in place looked thin. I phoned Kathy and told her what I thought and that the thin pegs could be trouble. Sure enough, off comes the net, easy because of the small pegs, and Russia gets the winner but it's called back and the game goes in to overtime.

T.J. Oshie, he never seems to miss. The USA uses him three times because you can use the same guy as many times as you want. T.J. sinks three goals in and the Russians are out. There goes their chance for a gold in hockey. The Russians got the most medals at the Olympics, except the one they wanted the most.

Putin was at the hockey games, not happy. It is so strange that the Russians always look bad in international hockey.

I asked Kathy if I could have a shot of the peg so I could show it on the next "Coach's Corner." She said she'd ask Toronto to get the shot which I thought was strange. Here we are in Russia, and we have to ask Toronto to get us the shot. (Remember I said at the start it would be better for me to stay in Toronto.)

I watch the Swedes beat Teddy Nolan's Latvia. Latvia looked good. Teddy almost pulled it off, but one of the Swedes made a perfect dive. (He should have gotten a ten sign for the dive). Sweden scored on a power play.

I noticed in the game that the captain of the Latvia club was not wearing a visor. I see Weber and Getzlaf who don't wear visors in the NHL wearing them in these games. I'm going to mention it to them next practice.

February 16, 2014. I woke up at six-thirty—can't believe it. I never sleep that long. I think it's starting to get to me. Bob Costas, the NBC announcer, got pinkeye and has to stay in the dark in the hotel room. The Russians have a great idea: when they are working on a building or the building does not look good, they wrap a large sheet around it, cover the whole building. It looks like it's complete with windows and doors unless you get up close. You would never know. I walked by twice, didn't notice. Tried to feed a little dog. Wouldn't eat, ran away. I don't think he's long for this world. I did not have the same bounce when I just came back here. Ron told me Trevor Pilling, the boss, said in the last game I came in like a hurricane full of life. He said there is hope for us, the way Don acts. I must admit I am wearing down a little. I never sleep all the way to six-thirty, even at home.

Canada plays Finland tonight, should be a better game. The last one against Austria was a joke. At twelve-fifteen, I went to the morning skate and made a mistake. Sent a message to Ryan Getzlaf that the captain of Latvia was not wearing a visor, thought he and another guy (Weber) might not have to wear one. It was only that old guys who played before certain dates don't have to wear a visor. Getzlaf and the rest are too young, must wear a visor according to the international rules. Watching the morning skate, found out they're starting Carey Price. Found out P.K. Subban and Martin St. Louis are not dressing. The best defence-man in the league and the best scorer in the league are not dressing. I watched the morning skate, and it's funny: when two guys get the shaft, they bond together. It's the same way on a team in the regular season. The guys who don't play form a clique and bond. I guess misery loves company. I know: I used to be one of the Black Aces, and we had our own little club.

I am going to tell Ron I am not going to do the opening bit from the studio. I used to like it in the playoffs when we were on the ice. There is nothing in the studio. I expect a hard time from Ron. I'm not feeling too well. I think a cold or something is coming on. See you after the game. We will beat Finland. I have to do my radio show, *The Grapeline*, in Kathy's room after the game. I am wearing a lion cap tonight. Wore a bear last night.

February 17, 2014. Toughed it out last night. My voice went, struggled through the night. Had to let on that nothing was wrong. Finished, had to go to Kathy's room to do *The Grapeline* with Brian (Williams). Really struggled there, did the best I could—not good. I am sitting in my room, just sitting here. I better be better tomorrow. Lucky I don't do anything till Wednesday—the quarter-finals. The hockey is awful for everybody. Five guys back, sit and wait for power plays or a break.

Can't think straight. Nose running, head spins. You don't miss your health till you get sick. Damn. Everything going along great till yesterday. Got to push through. It's that I meet so many people and shake hands. The odds are, I'm going to catch something.

February 18, 2014. Yesterday was a tough day. Never left the room, except to talk to Luba and Kathy. Slept in till 7:30 A.M. I never sleep that late. Feeling better—thank the Lord, because I do five straight games, including the women's gold Wednesday, Thursday, Friday, Saturday, Sunday at all hours. Going to say on "Coach's Corner" why they are going with Price instead of Luongo, and why so far Ovechkin, Malkin, Crosby, Perry and Getzlaf are not scoring. It has been raining. Lovely day today, got five games (I hope) in five days, plus radio shows after. I see I said that Russia beat

Latvia last night. Same game every game because of the big ice—you can't open up. If you do, you'll get caught. So what you do is bar the door—everybody back till you get a power play or get a break. The only time you open up is when you fall behind by three goals like Latvia did. Losing 4–1, they opened it up. Good game, almost won—4–3 and a chintzy penalty to Latvia. There is so little hitting—how about none. If you hit a guy, you're out of position, so when there is no hitting, the refs call what we call phantom penalties. When the whistle goes, everybody wonders who got it. It's sad to see teams lose on the chintzy penalties they call.

February 19, 2014. Good night's sleep, woke up around 6:30 A.M. Got a call from Kathy—can only talk about the game, the goalie and Ted Nolan. Going to say all his players understand English, that it's amazing here, all the announcements in English. All the games, even Russia versus Norway. All the Russians on TV, the people downtown speak it, saleslady, parking attendant. All the songs in figure skating in English, all English songs at the arena. A policeman said most Russians around here speak English.

February 20, 2014. We went to the women's morning skate and ended up at the wrong rink. It was a Russian practice. Did an interview with a female Russian reporter. We went to the other side of the rink to see the women's skate. I was the only media person there—everyone else was at the men's practice. I am glad I went. It seemed to give the women players a lift that somebody cared. In fact, one player tweeted she was glad to see Grapes there to give them encouragement. They waved after the practice. I gave them the thumbs up. I wished Kevin Dineen (their coach) good luck—they're going to need it. The U.S. team is good.

I met a reporter from Detroit for an interview. He told me the Russian reporters are a tough lot. One Russian reporter, in an interview with the Russian coach, said that if he plays a certain goalie, it's a death sentence (no kidding) and if he doesn't win the Olympics, he's disgraced all of Russia and he will be fired and sent to Siberia.

The game between the USA and Canadian women's teams was a barn burner. We were outplayed, but our goalie Shannon Szabados saved our Canadian bacon. She held us in there. We were down 2–0, but we came roaring back and tied it after Kevin pulled the goalie. There was a play where we were in their end, the puck came back to the point, the linesman gets in the way of the defense, the puck goes by and it trickles all the way down to the open net and hits the goalpost. If it goes in, it's all over, but we tie the game.

The game went into overtime. We get a cheap slashing penalty and it looked like it was over. They get a cheap call for slashing and we get a break—a U.S. player pulls down a Canadian on a breakaway and now it's four-on-three. Hayley Wickenheiser is in front, screening the goalie. Right-winger Rebecca Johnston feeds the puck to Laura Fortino in the corner and Fortino slides it over to Marie-Philip Poulin who puts it home for the winner. The Canadian women never quit—their heart came through again.

February 21, 2014. Going to the Canadian men's morning skate. Got to tough it out till the end. Have not missed a practice or a morning skate during the Olympics, and I'm proud of that. This has been a tough haul, but the women's gold medal win last night was worth the trip. At this morning's skate, three of our champions were there. Hayley Wickenheiser is really something. They took her captain's letter from her, but she never missed a beat, played terrific. This is her last Olympics. She made it a good one.

We beat the States 1–0 in the men's semifinal. We outshot them 37-30. Carey Price was terrific—he stood on his head. So was Jonathan Quick for the States.

Trevor Pilling, our boss, brought an interview I did before the Olympics with Perry Lefko where I said, "I guarantee we will win gold in the women's game and gold in the men's." It was in a magazine called *GoodLife Mississauga*.

Talked to Lu. There's an ice storm back home. She tells me they're going to allow bars to open early for the big game.

February 22, 2014. 3:10 P.M.: Went to the practice, did five interviews: French, Swedish, USA, Canada, Russia. The Swedes are all upset that there is a Canadian referee—they don't realize it's in their favour. I said, "I'll bet you anything you want that the Canadian ref will call a Canadian penalty first." That's the way we are; we bend over backwards to appease the other people. I remember when our figure skater Elizabeth Manley should have won a gold medal: Europeans and Americans wanted to reward her with the gold, but the one judge who ruled against her was the Canadian judge. That's just the way we are. I remember when I coached Team Canada in Sweden; the players were upset when they heard that we had a Canadian ref for the final game. They knew what was coming.

February 23, 2014. 8:10 P.M.: Canada won in a walk, 3–0. I really believe the way Coach Babcock played the four lines, we could have played another ten games. We were just warming up. Price was sensational, especially in the gold medal game. Doughty loved that big ice and was flying. But I've got to admit, I saw most of the games, if not in person, on the Russian TV, and except for a few games, especially the women's championship game, it was boring hockey with the big ice. As I said before, you can't hit because if you hit, you're out of position, and if you get a 1–0 lead, you sit back and it's "Katie, bar the door," play it safe, wait for a penalty or a break. If we gave that hockey in the NHL, we would be in trouble.

I remember when they asked Sundin how they could get more people at the games in Sweden he said they should make the rinks smaller and get more action. He's right, of course. I remember when I coached Team Canada back in the eighties. I went to a game between Finland and Sweden with my son, Tim. It looked for a 0–0 tie like soccer. I could read the program and never miss a beat, so we smoked the Swedes 3–0, no contest.

Kathy and Prior Smith, the producer of my radio show on 590 The Fan, had arranged for me to do the show with Brian Williams right after the game. We scooped everybody. I still don't know how they did it, but everyone at The Fan seemed happy.

The Russians would not allow buses or cars in the Olympic Park, so we had to walk through the park. My first time, the fireworks were just starting. It was beautiful. The Russians did a great job.

I was in Russia twenty-one days and I have to admit again, Russia was not what I expected. The Russian people tolerated us and some were friendly. It was clean, the people respected authority, but I noticed they did not smile a lot. Now here is the strange one: I did not see one fat Russian male the whole time I was there. The women were kind of heavy, but every guy looked in shape.

I finally made it back to my room, had a shower and sat to watch the closing ceremonies, the best ever. Who should knock on my door, but Ron. He somehow got off early. Great. The first time we have one of our sessions in three weeks, but I guess we were too tired to have a good session. We had a few and toasted that we survived. I don't know if "Coach's Corner" was good or not, but the suits were and Canada won both golds in hockey—that was the main thing.

February 24, 2014. 7:30 A.M.: Got a sore throat, still haven't confirmed about the truck to the airport. Lu phoned—I wasn't pleasant for some reason. Sometimes I wonder about myself. Like with Kevin Hunt, my friend since he was a kid with Tim—they went to school together and learned TV at Mohawk College. He helped me through the Olympics— he's the floor director, got me coffee, helped me with anything. I gave him a hard time about the chair I was sitting on. I know I hurt him—why would I give him and Lu a hard time? One I like, and one I love, and then I feel bad. Got a call from Kathy. She's in Moscow, a five-hour layover. The truck will be at the hotel at 4:15. Ron and I and Scott Russell and Jim Hughson are on it. What do we do without Kathy? She phones from Moscow to help—she is a blessing. I even gave her a hard time at the set. Meeting Ron in the sauna at eight-thirty. We better not drink too much—early start.

4:15 A.M. start and then an all-day, all-night trip. This is my last Olympics, even if the NHL goes to South Korea in 2018. The Russians did a wonderful job. They should be proud. Better than Salt Lake, better than the one in Japan. Clean, polite, well-run under difficult circumstances.

They got the most medals, but to make a complete success at the Games, they had to win the hockey gold. That was the main sport for President Putin. I can't figure out why Russia always plays so bad in international hockey. They scored one goal.

The weather has been fantastic. It's like a beautiful fall day. Lu says there is so much ice at home, you can't walk. Nevertheless, I will be happy to get to the weather at home, ice and all.

February 25, 2014. 4:35 P.M.: We make it home. Lu has a little can of beer with the little umbrella in it, saying, "Welcome home," sitting on the doorstep. Inside are four balloons saying HAPPY BIRTHDAY! as I spent my eightieth in Russia. Lu says, "How was it?"

"Piece of cake."

February 26, 2014. Spent most of the day resting and doing interviews, unpacking.

February 27, 2014. Glad to be home. Start packing to go to Vancouver for the Heritage Game.

February 28, 2014. Fly to Vancouver for the Heritage Game. It seems we're living in airplanes.

March 1, 2014. It's Saturday night, so we have to do "Coach's Corner" for the Montreal game back east. We go to the Heritage Game site. They are just setting up and the place is empty and people are wandering around. We did "Coach's Corner" and weren't satisfied, but we did our best under the circumstances.

March 2, 2014. Up in the morning. We have a room to go to for breakfast, but we never go. Ron orders room service and I have my usual breakfast, first Lu's bran muffin and then some oatmeal. Off we go to the Heritage Game.

It's always turmoil at these games, pushing and shoving. We do the opening, which is mediocre at best, but we did our best. Watch the first period. I cannot believe how the Vancouver coach is not starting his number one goalie, Roberto Luongo. He lets Roberto sit as the back-up goalie. I know Roberto is fuming. Imagine. He's a guy who took the Vancouver club to the Stanley Cup final and one game away from the Stanley Cup he is embarrassed like this in front of 50,000 of his fans. He already had a slap in the face that Price played in the Olympics after he won the gold in 2010 at home. (Price was sensational in the Olympics, so it was the right move.)

Right now, it was tough on Roberto. Now he comes

home feeling like he can show everybody they were wrong and he's told that he won't be playing in the Heritage Game. I said on "Coach's Corner" it was a big mistake. The Canucks just lost their goalie. I knew the coach would be gone and I knew GM Mike Gillis would be gone. That was a dumb move. The only hope for the Canucks to make the playoffs was a hot Luongo, and as you know, no playoffs for the Canucks, Gillis is gone and Tortorella is gone. I really believe if they had played Roberto that game and kept playing him the Canucks would have made it to the playoffs and Gillis and Tortorella would still be there. Why? Because Luongo had something to prove and there is nothing like a guy who is on a mission to prove people wrong.

We do "Coach's Corner." It's not very good. (Hey, you can't win them all. Some nights you have it and sometimes it's not there. I can't explain it. For some reason, this is one of those nights. I miss my studio with the little red light on the camera and darkness.)

We make our way back to the hotel through the crowd. I am alone this night—Ron goes out with friends. I never go out. I love being in my room alone, having a few pops, watching the baseball or the hockey game. I know it doesn't sound good that I like drinking alone. Cold Buds, peanuts, popcorn and cheese are heaven to me.

We're up early for the flight back to Toronto. I meet with the boss of Rogers Sportsnet, Scott Moore at 8:00 A.M. and he tells me what's going to happen next year with *Hockey Night in Canada*. Doesn't seem to affect "Coach's Corner." I guess he just wanted to get things straight with me.

I knock on Ron's door. He's feeling a little rocky as he stayed up late with the NHL alumni. He's in a little bit of shock, too, as he's been told he will not be doing the host job for *Hockey Night in Canada*, but is still on "Coach's Corner" and a new gig *Hometown Hockey* or something that's every Sunday night. He will be great just like he's great on *Hockey Day in Canada* and *Hockeyville*. He doesn't say much about it. I think he's still in shock. I think he's exhausted from the Olympics, too. He had a schedule that would kill a horse. At the Olympics, we would do "Coach's Corner" after he did a half-hour pre-game show and then he would do fifteen minutes before the opening and then "Coach's Corner," the panel between the second and third periods, do the wrap-up at the end of the third period and then do highlights for back home on CBC. He'd then go back to the Sochi media building and work all night on the Olympics, catch a few hours of sleep, work all afternoon, catch a few more hours of sleep and start all over again with the game that night. He did this for twenty-one straight days. No wonder he slept all the way back to Toronto.

As we are boarding the plane home from Vancouver, we are greeted by a buddy of mine, Brian Bellows. He is the head steward. Brian reminds me of the time when he thought he was a hockey player and tried out for the Rochester Americans when I was GM and coach. Brian was one of the players. One day, he came to me and said, "Don, I want your honest opinion. I have a chance to go with Air Canada for a job, but I want to be a hockey player. What do you think I should do?"

I said, "Brian, take the Air Canada job. It is a good job, steady. You don't want to end up like me in the American Hockey League, riding the buses for twenty years and, at the end, have no job. Be smart. You're a pretty good player, but you are an AHLer like me. You could make our club, but Air Canada is solid." And he has a great job. I guess, in a few years, a pension. He was a lot smarter than me.

We get home, and I am slowly wearing down. And for some reason, my wrist is killing me. In bed again.

March 4, 2014. Next day, like a fool, I scheduled a banquet without Lu's knowledge. I told you I wasn't too bright. Luckily, Cindy says she will drive me. It's a luncheon for Domino's Pizza. We leave at 5:45 P.M. and make it. The Windsor Casino people are great, there are three hundred people, meet them and take pictures. Do banquet, great audience. Drive back. It's been a tough month. Cindy drops me off. I go to bed—I don't even have a pop. Thank you, Lord, for getting me through this month. I enjoyed the Olympics, but it is my last forever. I will be smarter in the future about banquets. I'm going to have to stop thinking I'm still thirty-two years old. Maybe thirty-five years old. That sounds right.

MUSINGS

I OFTEN WONDER WHAT WAS in my makeup that made Eddie Shore hate me so much. Let me explain about Eddie. A famous player, tough as nails for the Boston Bruins, he won the Hart Trophy three times, but when he retired, he was a tyrant. He was a hard man with no mercy, ruined hockey players and lives. He was hated so much and feared that players had it in their contracts that they could not be sent to the Springfield Indians in the American Hockey League.

The Indians were a good hockey team—won three Calder Cup championships—but it was the Alcatraz of hockey. To play there, you must be desperate. It was torture. Eddie thought up ways to harass the players, and for some reason he hated me the most. I really never knew why. He sent me to Three Rivers, Quebec, at Christmas one year. The next year, he traded me at Christmas to the Sudbury Wolves of the Eastern Professional Hockey League. I remember when I got the news that I was going to a lower league, the guys were jealous that I was escaping the prison, but I never did find out why the hate for me.

I was number one on his list to harass. I never gave him a hard time, I never argued with him. It was strange. I never did find out till a couple of years ago.

My daughter, Cindy, was talking to Brian Kilrea at a hockey game one night. Kilrea was the coach of the Ottawa 67's, the winningest junior coach of all time, and played with me on the Springfield Indians.

Cindy says Brian reminds her more of me than any other person, so Cindy said, "Brian, you and Dad are alike. How come Mr. Shore liked you and hated Dad?"

Yes, Shore did like Brian until Brian led the strike against him, which finally drove Eddie out of hockey, so Brian was no suck. He gave Eddie a hard time and argued with him, but Eddie liked him from the first day and Brian liked Eddie. Brian likes Eddie to this day. So what was it that made Eddie take an instant dislike for me—and for that matter, his coach, Pat Egan, couldn't stand me, either. It was like scenes out of a movie. Suspended for indifferent play when I hadn't played in a week. Suspended for something twenty other guys did and they got no suspension or fine. Always with the Black Aces. The Black Aces were the guys who were in trouble and always being punished. One time I spent four and a half hours on the ice after practice. (It's funny, everybody thought my feet would hurt. No, it was my back that hurt.)

When my cheque came for winning the Calder Cup, it was cut in half. The other players got half of my cheque, and still he never let up in practice. I set a record for being called out five times in three minutes. Always screaming, "Mr. Cherry, bend those knees, hold that stick right!" It never stopped. One time, I took one stride on the ice, while pulling on my gloves, and he screamed about the way I skated.

Kent Douglas—who went on to glory with the Toronto Maple Leafs, got Rookie of the Year—and others used to argue with Eddie all the time. And then other players used to suck up to him. Now that I think of it, I was the guy in no-man's-land, never argued (which he seemed to like) or sucked up to him (which he seemed to like). He would literally scream at me, "Mr. Cherry, in most hands, a hockey stick is a scientific tool. In yours, it's a blunt instrument." (I must admit, I did tend to use it to straighten guys out.) And of course, the beauty: "Mr. Cherry, if you could visualize that in reality your manoeuvrability is nil!" I always liked that one. I guess he didn't like the way I skated. He loved guys like Brian that skated with their knees bent. Unfortunately, I skated stiff-legged. The more he hollered at me, the more I clammed up, just stood there and looked at him. When he said, "You have anything to say?" I just looked at him.

Brian's answer to Cindy on why Mr. Shore took a particular dislike to me was, "It's funny you ask that, Cindy. I ask Eddie one day after your dad had left, 'Eddie, why was it that you had it in for Don Cherry?' Eddie told me that it really pissed him off that I stood there with a look of insolence on my face. 'Cherry never said a word back, but that look of insolence on his face said it all.'"

The story I am going to tell now concerns a program that was on a few years ago. It was called *Who Do You Think You Are?* It was a show that dealt with your past. I travelled to France to visit the grave of my relative, Sergeant Thomas

William Mackenzie (military medal and bar), who was killed in the First World War, on November 7, 1918, just days before the war would end, and to Vimy Ridge, to honour my grandfather, Richard Palamountain. These fellows were on the side of my mother.

The show also wanted to show my father's side. They showed my grandfather, John T. Cherry, who was a captain of a ship called the *Holcomb*, out of Kingston for the Canadian Steamship Line. John T. sailed the St. Lawrence River and Lake Ontario for twenty-two years—never had an accident or wreck. When he was seventeen, he joined the army and fought the U.S. in the Fenian raids when the U.S. invaded Canada. He later joined the North-West Mounted Police (now the RCMP) at the time the Americans from Montana were coming up to Canada with rotgut whisky and trading it for furs, horses and food from the Indians, and the Indians were starving when winter came.

Sir John A. Macdonald, the prime minister, called for volunteers to straighten out the Yanks and save the Indians. They made a march of eight hundred miles through dense bush and over barren prairies, starving and freezing. They started with 150 horses and ended up with fifty. It was one of the hardest journeys I have ever read about. John T. joined at nineteen. I know, reader, you're thinking, "What has this to do with Eddie Shore and your problem?" Kindly read on, please.

I am a great reader of military history and the military ways. In one interesting book, there was a chapter on how you could be court-martialled, put in prison or what. One way that caught my eye for a soldier to be put in prison or court-martialled was for "silent insolence." Imagine a soldier in prison for not saying a word, just the way he looked. I guess Eddie Shore knew what he was talking about with my attitude and my face. In the military rules, it described insolence as to stand and face the officer, not saying a word, but having the look of detachment and disdain on the soldier's face. It is a look not to gain popularity, and I guess that is why Eddie could not stand me. Believe me, folks, I caused my family a lot of grief with that look, but looking back, I'm sure I would do it again. You are what you are, and I guess I was just asking for it.

I know what you're saying: "What has my problem with Eddie Shore got to do with my grandfather, John. T. Cherry?" The producers of *Who Do You Think You Are?* wanted me to see John T. Cherry's record in the North-West Mounted Police, so they had a representative of the Mounties come to RMC in Kingston. As you know, RMC is the West Point of Canada—or West Point is the RMC of the U.S. The gentleman met me in a very austere room filled with books and low lights, lovely cherry wood. He stood with white gloves on and a book before him. After formal introductions, he explained that this book contained the records of the famous march west, including John T.'s record in the military.

With all the heroes and generals looking down on us from the pictures on the walls, he explained that the march was so hard, the regiment had a lot of deserters. They just left as they neared the U.S. border. They just went down to the States, but John T. stuck it out to the bitter end and stopped the whisky traders and stayed in the service for three years. He was offered 180 acres in Saskatchewan, but decided to come back to Kingston. John T.'s record shows he had problems with the discipline of the military in the first months. He made only seventy-five cents a day. He was fined three dollars for letting a horse get loose and five dollars for riding on a cart. And then the gentleman from Ottawa read the last fine, for a whopping fifteen dollars. He looked up at me and said, "You know, Mr. Cherry, as I read these fines, I can see the acorn never fell far from the tree. Take a look at what your grandfather was fined fifteen dollars for." As I looked at the page, he pointed to one word.

Insolence.

John T. straightened out after the first month and was never fined or disciplined again. I'm sure he would have wanted me to let you know.

* * *

When I hear a Canadian franchise in any sport complain they can't get any free-agent stars to sign in a Canadian city, I think of the four basketball players that were traded from Sacramento, California, to the Toronto Raptors in 2013. They were traded to Toronto in the middle of December. Think about the players. They just left sunny California, walking around in shorts, enjoying life. They are called in. "You have been traded to the Raptors in Toronto."

Jump ahead, they're in shock. Going to live in Canada, they are on the plane to Toronto. They are looking down at

Toronto in the middle of a severe snowstorm. I can hear
them now. "Are you kidding me? I have to live *here* for six
months? Look at that snow! How do they live up here?
What did we do to deserve this?" And if you remember, the
snow just kept comin'.

Now, I know the Sacramento team is not full of stars and
they suck, but really, where do you think those players would
rather play: the frozen North or lovely Sacramento in the
summer breezes? If you're going to miss the playoffs, miss
them in a place you enjoy and a country you understand.

The Blue Jays did sign a lot of baseball stars, but overpaid
everybody to get them to come to Canada.

The Maple Leafs will never get a superstar to come here
for a lot of reasons. First, the stars want to go where they win
or have a good shot at the Stanley Cup. They can go to
someplace like San Jose, Anaheim or Chicago and get lost
in the crowd. Their families would love the weather in L.A.,
Anaheim and San Jose.

The baseball and basketball players have no idea about
Canada. I have to say it, but I lived down in the States from
when I was nineteen, in 1954, till I came back in 1980. I
came back to Kingston to work on construction, but left
after a while. I stayed in the States after I got married to a
girl from the States, Rose. She and her family had no idea
about Canada. Imagine, a six-hour dive from Hershey,
Pennsylvania, to Kingston. It was unbelievable.

I asked Rose one day, "In school, did you ever learn about
Canada?"

She said, "Not a word about Canada. We learned all about
South America and its capitals, but nothing about Canada."

It used to bug me.

When I married Rose and brought her back to Kingston, as we left for the trip north, her mother, God bless her, said, "Now remember, Rosemarie, when you come to the border, put on your sweater."

I was listening to the Carolina Hurricanes' hockey broadcast the other night and the U.S. announcer said so-and-so come home from a small little city in Canada: Regina, Saskatchewan. I guess the Canadian colour guy agreed. He didn't want the U.S. announcer to look bad. But what was the difference? Nobody knew the difference.

Hey, don't get me wrong. I never, ever heard an American knock Canada. They always had nice things to say about us. They knew a little. Canadians back then were very polite. We had very little crime to speak of. Of course, that's all changed now, but that's a whole new story. But back to the basketball players from Sacramento.

They get off the plane, they have to wait in those four-mile-long lines at customs, which they're going to have to go through when they fly to the States. They finally get through and they wait for their bags. They finally get outside; it's freezing and a snowstorm. They see a sign and they ask, "What the heck is a millimetre?" And another sign, it says NORD and SUD. "What the hell are 'nord' and 'sud' and 'sortie'?" They walk outside in the blinding snowstorm and think, "What the heck did we do to deserve this?" and dream of the warm, sunny breezes in Sacramento.

* * *

I am with my son, Tim, who rates the kids in minor midget for the Ontario Hockey League. We are watching the Junior Canadians and the Mississauga Rebels. I am having fun. When the whistle stops, I'm signing sticks, posing for pictures—it seems every kid has a camera now with those phones, guys and girls, seven and eight years old, working magic on them. I'm just getting into touch phones. I have no cell phone, have no idea about texting and stuff. My wife, Luba, was a private secretary so she is an expert on that stuff.

I must admit I'm lost when it comes to emails and stuff—not like Ron MacLean, who is really into emails like my son, Tim, who at this game asks into his phone who won the game between Columbus and Philly, and it answers him. Amazing!

I know some of you are saying, "Yeah, but you're on Twitter." Let me explain. In the playoffs two years ago, the boss of *Hockey Night in Canada*, Trevor Pilling, and Kathy Broderick, the producer who runs "Coach's Corner," convinced me.

(If you want to find out what's going on at CBC, just ask Kathy. One time, I told her, "Kathy, if they ever get rid of you, I'm quitting." Kathy said, "Gee, Grapes, please don't tell them that." She's also a wise guy.)

They told me that there were about five guys using my name on the Twitter, making statements, and people think *I* was making the statements. I told them I knew nothing about Twitter. Kathy said she would take care of it, that I just needed to phone her and she would put what I want to say on Twitter.

I told them I had no problem with guys imitating me—in fact, there's a guy out there who imitates me who's got me down perfect. He does banquets, even went on *Dragons' Den* for money to expand his operations. Trevor and Kathy said this Twitter is different. CBC had to protect itself and me because those guys were saying things that were libel.

* * *

I have come to a conclusion: I'm still a minor leaguer in many ways after all these years. For instance, there's the guilty feeling I have when I fly first class. I remember when I was with the Bruins, I would force Jean Ratelle to take my place in first class. Don't get me wrong, I enjoy it, but I have a funny feeling when first-class passengers gets on the plane first. I wonder what the people think as we get on.

I say to Ron, "We don't need a limo. Let's take a cab."

Yeah, I know, what you're thinking. All those fancy suits and jackets. Honestly, I treat them as costumes. I feel more at home with a T-shirt, cut-off sleeves and Crazeewear pants.

I feel a bond when I drive past guys on a construction site, especially if a guy is on a jackhammer. I always say to Ron as we drive by in our limo, "I did that. I love those guys." Ron always says, "Yeah! Yeah! I know. You've told me a thousand times." I did it for so long, my ears have a noise permanently, there all the time, like one of those bugs you hear on a hot day in the summer. The doctor told me there is no cure.

I live in a small house. The kids at Halloween say, "Hey, it's Don Cherry! You live in this small house?" Out of the mouths of babes.

I drive a '93 Ford F-150 pickup and a 1983 Lincoln.

I still can't believe people want their picture taken with me or my autograph. Like I said earlier, I feel if I was off TV for a year, people would say when they meet me, "Didn't you use to be Don Cherry?"

When I coached the Bruins, Harry Sinden, the GM, ordered breakfast with me one day and he ordered orange juice—a little glass of it cost a dollar fifty. I didn't order any. He said, "How come you don't want orange juice?"

"Not at a dollar fifty for that small glass," I replied.

Harry said, "You can take the minor leaguer out of the minor leagues, but you can't take the minor leagues out of the minor leaguer." That saying came back to me when Ron ordered a $2.50 glass of orange juice the other day. (Again, I didn't have any.) Even when the orange juice is free I won't have it. It would not be right.

When I go on the road, Luba makes me salmon sandwiches, and for breakfast I have my All-Bran and Luba's muffins, even though I could go to a special room for free breakfast. I always remember my Scotch grandmother, Maggie Mackenzie. She used to lecture me. One of her sayings was "Any fool can make money; it's the wise one that saves it."

I do not enjoy myself the way Ron does. I admire him in a way. He travels all over the world. He buys first-class clothes and new cars. When we are in the playoffs and he goes and exercises, or for a swim, he looks like he stepped out of *Vogue* magazine. He buys those expensive magazines that cost $7.95 and ten dollars and reads them and leaves them on the plane. Imagine.

The point I'm trying to make in my inept way is that all those years I spent in the minor leagues, where I earned $4500 for ten years, our road money was $4.00 a day with the feelings of being unemployed never leaving my thoughts. I'm not cheap, I pay my rounds. Sammy Pollock, when he was GM of Montreal, kept a book on everybody. When Sammy put my name in the book, he only wrote three words:

Confirmed Minor Leaguer.

And Sammy was right.

THE GOOD OLD DAYS

WHEN I'M ON A RADIO TALK SHOW or when I'm at a banquet, I'm often asked one interesting question, and the question is, "Don, in all your career in the minor leagues, what player do you think should have been in the NHL and was down with you in the minors?" I could have answered a lot of guys, like Billy Sweeney, playing for the Springfield Indians. Billy won three scoring titles in a row, over a hundred points in sixty-some games and three championships. He was owned by Eddie Shore and never got a shot at the show.

Another player who was buried in the minors, because the Toronto Maple Leafs were ticked off at him for some reason or the other—I never found out why—was Frank Mathers. When he played for the Pittsburgh Hornets against the Hershey Bears of the AHL, I was a rookie. When I saw him playing in the minors, I said, "If *he* can't make the NHL, who can?" He was sensational. An All-Star every year. But folks, you have to realize there were only six teams in the NHL and they only carried five defencemen apiece.

That means there were only thirty defencemen in the NHL. Today, they carry seven defencemen, some eight defencemen, so say they have thirty teams—that's 210 defencemen in the NHL now, compared with only thirty before. And the teams back in those days only carried one goalie, so that means that there was six goalies in the NHL. Now they carry two goalies, so that means that there are 60 goalies in the NHL. And back then, they only carried ten forwards, which means there were only eighty, ninety forwards in the NHL. Now there are over four hundred forwards in the NHL. So you can see, it was slim pickings if you got in the bad books and never got out of the bad books. Figure it out. There were six teams in the NHL, six teams in the AHL, six teams in the Western Hockey League and six teams in the Central Hockey League. That would have been all the professional teams in the world. So combine the three pro leagues. That means that there were twenty-four teams, compared to now: there are thirty teams just in the NHL.

All of us playing in the minors in those days would be playing in the NHL, and we could have had another six teams to fill. The Boston Bruins put me in the doghouse, never to get out, when they told me not to play baseball in the summer. I love baseball and, like a fool, played against their wishes and broke my shoulder. They showed their displeasure and sent me to the dregs of society and the Siberia of hockey, the Springfield Indians of the AHL and Eddie Shore. That was at the age of twenty-two, and I was doomed to the next twenty years in the minors. And a million miles on the buses. I paid the price.

Yes, there were a lot of good hockey players also doomed to the minors like me, for some infraction or the other. Also, another reason a lot of guys never made it: for instance, they would bring up a guy who was an offensive talent and he'd be on the fourth line and never on the power play. And he would be sent down, with the team saying he could score in the AHL but not in the NHL. The real reason he didn't score is they didn't give him a chance and he became another confirmed minor, like me.

I can name tons of guys who got the shaft, but the one guy who I thought got the biggest shaft of all was a nifty player called Guyle Fielder. He was born in the U.S., I remember, but grew up in Nipawin, Saskatchewan. I have to say, he was a sensational hockey player. He ticked some-body off—again, I never found out who he ticked off, but he was one of us in the minor leagues his whole life. Chicago signed him when he was fifteen years old but released him. Guyle ended up with Detroit, played on the fourth line, hardly hitting the ice. The following year, he was sent to Boston. Same thing, and back to Detroit the next year. Jack Adams, GM and coach, put him between Ted Lindsay and Gordie Howe. As you know, Lindsay and Howe liked the puck and they liked to handle the puck. And they would. Now, Guyle liked to handle the puck, too. Detroit lost six straight, and guess who was benched? Not Lindsay and Howe. Guyle went to Jack Adams's office and said he would like to play. And Adams said he would play, all right, but he sent him to the WHL to Seattle to play. And he did for the next twelve years. And that's when I saw him play. I was playing for the Spokane Comets, and believe me, he was a magician with the puck. Okay, his skating wasn't Bobby Orr's, but whose was? But he got there. When he was on the ice, you had to be aware and keep your eye on him all the time. He could fool you in a dozen ways. And around the net, he would appear out of nowhere and pop it in. Like I said, he was a magician.

Imagine! He won eleven scoring titles, nine in the WHL, which is just a step below the NHL, and never got a shot. Yeah, I know what you are thinking: "You were a minor leaguer too! That's why you think another minor leaguer is great. How would you know a good or bad NHLer?" Well, let me tell you this: I was at every training camp in the NHL for a couple of weeks, I will say, so I saw them all play. All the stars. I played against them, I scrimmaged with them, I played exhibition games with them. Mind you, I didn't stay long, but I played against them—I played against all the stars—so I had a good idea what a hockey player was, and I knew a good hockey player from a bad hockey player.

So my answer to the question, "Who got the biggest shaft from the NHL and was buried in the minors?" No doubt it was Guyle "The Golden Guyle" Fielder. I figure he would be making about eight million a year in the NHL right now. Talk about being born in the wrong time!

* * *

I have seen a lot of hockey players who were great ruin their life with drinking, but the greatest I ever saw was a player back in the fifties, Réal Chevrefils.

When I first saw him, I got the same feeling as when I saw Bobby Orr. How does he skate so well and handle the puck so effortlessly? Now, he wasn't in Bobby's class, but he was an amazing player. His junior coach, Hap Emms, the GM and coach of the Barrie Flyers, called him the greatest prospect for the NHL he'd ever seen.

Réal played for the Flyers. In his last season with the Flyers, he scored 52 goals and 51 assists in only 54 games, and he was tough, too. Over a hundred minutes in penalties, he was a sensation. Réal was Boston Bruins property and they could hardly wait to get him—a bright future was ahead. He was one of those guys the scouts say "can't miss," but dark clouds were on the horizon behind this great prospect.

Réal was one of those guys who kept the dressing room laughing with jokes and imitations. Everybody loved him, even on the ice. When he'd score, he'd make a funny voice, "WOO-EEE!" He was fun to be around and he produced. In 1956–57 he scored 31 goals when 30 was a wonder. He was an All-Star three times, but the dark clouds that were forming turned into a storm. His love of alcohol overcame his love for hockey, and it was sad to see this great—and I mean *great*—downfall. And his fall was fast. The year after he scored 31 goals, the Bruins sent him to the minors to teach him a lesson and to dry out. Of all the places to send him: the Springfield Indians, the Siberia of hockey, where I was toiling for Eddie Shore. We did everything we could to help him. We gave up beer so he had no temptations. He was such a warm, funny guy. We were rooting for him all the way. Réal was doing great and playing great. In fifteen games, he had seven goals and eight assists and he was dry as bones. We were proud of him and we knew it was only a matter of time until he was back to the show.

Then, disaster. He was persuaded by some of his so-called friends from Boston to drive there to see a game. We did everything we could to stop him because we knew: once he got in that crowd, it was over. He went to Boston, got with his old cronies and went to the game drinking. It was the end, and we knew it. One guy on the Springfield club, when he heard the news, broke down crying. He was thinking of Réal's wife and kids. It was a fast spiral down. He went to the AHL, was sent to the Quebec League, then to the EPHL, then to the WHL, and finally ended up in senior hockey. From All-Star to senior hockey in a couple of years.

I won't dwell on his final days. He lost everything—wife, kids, reputation—and he died young, but you know, till the day he died, everybody loved him. I never saw him play in the final years, I only saw him play when he was great, and I will never forget the first time I saw him at the Boston camp and watched him handle a puck and skate. Man, I said to myself, this is a hockey player.

* * *

I know players now who played for Eddie Shore, the Darth Vader of hockey, who still talk about how great Eddie was. As a player, he might've been second only to Bobby Orr, and I will admit, at age sixty-two he could skate like the wind, but I am not one of the players that speak glowing of Eddie. I really feel he was a little off-balance, to say the least. Let me tell you a story, and you decide.

The Springfield Indians of the AHL had training camp at Niagara Falls, Ontario, where we trained for four weeks (with no pay), twice a day, and once, when he was mad at us, three practices in one day. It was a tough struggle, but we had to put up with it.

One day, a young boy showed up. He had taken the bus all the way from Springfield, Massachusetts, to be with us in Niagara Falls. He loved the club and would sit in the stands and watch the practices. I befriended the kid. He was having a tough time, as he was, shall we say, a little slow. He never bothered anybody and was very polite. After practice one day, I was a little late, as I had to stay to get ice on an injury from stopping a puck with my ankle. The arena was empty, and as I walked by this one room, I heard a whimper. I looked in, and it was the room where the trainer kept the sticks. The sticks were kept in a heavy wire enclosure, protected by heavy locks so nobody could get into the sticks to steal them. It was dark, and I still heard the whimper. As my eyes became accustomed to the dark I saw, there on the floor of the stick room, was the kid from Springfield. I knew exactly what happened. Some of the players had locked him in there and forgotten about him. I went to find the manager of the rink to let him out. I felt terrible that this poor kid had travelled all that way and got treated like this. What must he be thinking about hockey players?

I decided I must do something. I collected two dollars from every player, went to a sports store and bought a beauty sport jacket. Talked to the trainer to see if he had anything I could put on the jacket, and he just happened to have a beautiful Springfield crest. I took the jacket and crest to a shoemaker and asked him if he could sew the crest on the jacket. He did, and before supper with the team, which I invited the boy to, I presented him with the jacket. He got teary as he accepted the jacket while we cheered and clapped and sang, "For He's a Jolly Good Fellow." He was the happiest kid in the whole world when he put the jacket on.

I noticed Eddie, staying in a corner, with the usual frown on his face.

That night, I had a knock on my door. The coach, Pat Egan, said, "Eddie wants to see you in his room."

I said, "What about?"

He said, "You'll see."

I knocked on his door, went inside, and he sat there, glowering at me. "What made you buy that jacket for that kid?"

I couldn't tell him that I did it to make up for some jerks that locked him in the stick room, so I said, "He's a nice boy. He travelled all the way from Springfield to visit us and I thought he would like it."

He said, "Do you think you're fooling me? You bought him that jacket and gave it to him because you burned his jacket."

I looked at him to see if he was serious or if he was just fooling. I should have known he never fooled. I said, "Ed, why would you think my story's not true?"

"Quit your lying, I know it's true."

I could see there was no use arguing with Eddie. He had made up his mind I had burned the kid's jacket. I never did find out why he thought that.

I said to Eddie, "Well, Eddie, think what you like," and as

I turned to leave, the door was closing when he hollered, "You'll pay for that, Cherry!" And Eddie made sure that I did.

* * *

I would like to tell you about a beauty guy by the name of Garnet "Ace" Bailey. He was named Ace after the great Hall of Famer who played for the Toronto Maple Leafs, Irvine "Ace" Bailey, who was almost killed by Boston's Eddie Shore in a game at the Boston Garden in 1933.

Born in Lloydminster, Saskatchewan, in 1948, the younger Ace played junior for the Edmonton Oil Kings. In 56 games, he had 47 goals and 46 assists. Turned pro with the Boston Bruins in 1968–69. In eight games, got three goals and three assists. Imagine, six points in eight games and they sent him down to the minors! Boston did not have good teams. I still wonder why they sent him down. In the minors, in Hershey of the American League, he scored 24 goals and 32 assists in 60 games. Did great in the playoffs, 9 goals in 10 games. For the rest of his career, he hit the road: Boston (where everybody remembers him), then Detroit, St Louis, Washington, Edmonton in the World Hockey Association, then the Central Hockey League—Houston Apollos, Wichita Wind. So Ace paid his dues in hockey, but he did something in his career that not many people did: he played with Bobby Orr and Wayne Gretzky.

That's Ace's background, but Ace's life was so much more, and yes, I know, when a guy dies, usually people say he was a good guy. But let me tell you, folks, he was a treasure. Honestly, he always had a smile on his face, always had a good word for everybody. I know what you're thinking: too good to be true. It's true.

I will admit, when he was young, he was wild. He was a buddy of a young Wayne Cashman, and they had fun. One story goes that they were both sent down to Hershey of the AHL from Boston. It took them two days of driving to get there. In the Hershey arena, you can drive into the building and onto the ice. The team was just coming on the ice for practice. Ace and Wayne drove out onto the middle of the ice and said to the coach, "Well, we're here, coach, ready to go." Like I said, he was a teammate and good friend of Bobby Orr and a teammate and good friend of Wayne Gretzky.

Ace was a third- and fourth-line guy who was a penalty killer and a stir-'em-up guy. He was also a great character guy in the dressing room. He was one of those guys, if somebody new came to the team, he would be the first to welcome them. He was especially good with rookies. Wayne and Ace were very close. Wayne told me that when he and Ace were in the World Hockey Association, one night they went with a friend to the Boston Bruins' game in the Garden—we were playing the Philadelphia Flyers that night. It was one of our usual games we always had with the Flyers—no prisoners. Wayne said to Ace, when they were driving in the car back to their hotel, "I never will be able to play in that league. I'm too small." Ace gave him heck and said, "Shut up, Gretz, you'll play in the NHL and you'll be a star."

Wayne said one time in a game, there was this one player running around and trying to hurt him. He said something to Ace and Ace said, "Next time you're on with him, steer him over to the bench where I'm sitting." So sure enough, this guy starts chasing Wayne, so Wayne skates alongside his bench with this guy following. He hears a *whomp*, looks back and the guy is lying on the ice out cold. Ace cold-clocked him.

Ace always wore a white turtleneck on the ice and had a lot of time on the bench, as most third- and fourth-line guys do. But sometimes those guys are as important as your first and second lines. For instance, I remember in the 1972 finals, the Boston Bruins were playing the New York Rangers. The Bruins took a big lead in the first game, 5–1, but the Rangers tied the game and things looked bad for the Bruins. Tom Johnson, the Bruins coach, benched Eddie Westfall and put Ace in in his spot. Ace had barely played in the game, so his legs were ice cold, he told me, but he received a beauty pass from Shakey Walton and cut around the defence and put one in the top shelf past Hall of Famer Eddie Giacomin for a 6–5 win on their way to a Stanley Cup. If the Rangers had won that first game with a comeback like that, they would have been tough to beat. But Orr turned his magic on and the Bruins won the Cup. The coach and GM of the Rangers, Emile Francis, said after the series, "We could beat the Bruins, but we couldn't beat Bobby Orr. He was in another league."

Ace, after he retired, become a coach in the minors with Wichita and Houston. He went with the Edmonton Oilers as a scout for twelve years. Ace went to the L.A. Kings and became director of pro scouting, but his heart was always with the Boston Bruins, and he lived in Boston.

We will always remember this date: September 11, 2001. Ace and his buddy Mark Bavis were both scouting for the

L.A. Kings. Ace was teaching the young Bavis the tricks on scouting. They both had slept in and had to catch the plane to L.A. They made it to Logan Airport, seemed to hit all green lights, raced to the gate and just made it as they were closing the gates, thank their lucky stars. And as you will all remember, the plane was hijacked and flown into the World Trade Center.

I often think of "what ifs." What if Mark and Ace had slept five minutes longer? What if Ace had said, "We'll catch the next flight, Mark." What if they hadn't hit all of those green lights? If only they had been delayed five minutes somewhere . . . but I guess life is not made of "what ifs."

I can still see Ace with his white turtleneck, smiling, saying, "How's it going, Grapes?" Like I said earlier, he was a great guy and I'll always remember him.

* * *

I know there have been stories written and things said on TV about the famous (or infamous) too-many-men-on-the-ice incident in Boston back in 1979. The one that cost us a shot at the Cup. When a team nowadays has too many men on the ice, they bring up that game. Michael Farber of *Sports Illustrated* said he can't think of a more crushing mistake in sports, in any sport.

I've got to admit, I have to agree. It was a dynamite game. I remember Tie Domi telling me a few years ago about the Leafs flying to Florida after a game. They got in about 3:00 A.M. and were all still pumped up from the game. They all turned on ESPN, which had the '79 game on.

Usually in hotels, the team has a whole floor booked just for them. Every door was open, and the whole team watched the game.

Tie said the players couldn't believe the speed of some of the guys and the hard hitting. And what a game. I am going to give you the whole story about that game and about how I felt and how the players felt.

It would be funny if it wasn't so sad that everyone who follows hockey remembers the goal that Guy Lafleur scored against the Boston Bruins in the seventh game with Boston leading by one goal. There was 1:43 left in the game—this was the semifinals, but really, it was for the Stanley Cup, because the New York Rangers were already in the finals, waiting for the winner of this series. Beating New York would be a piece of cake for either Boston or Montreal, so this game was for all the marbles.

We only had 1:43 to go. We had played a great game, especially Gilly Gilbert, our so-called backup goalie for Gerry Cheevers. I had made the decision to go with Gilly after Gerry had lost the first two in Montreal, for a couple of reasons. Number one: he was a good goalie. He set a record for winning seventeen straight games in a row, a record that still stands. Number two: his contract was coming up. Number three: he was a French guy. He would have loved to beat Montreal, and if I hadn't goofed up with too many men on the ice, we would have beaten them.

The Montreal Canadiens of that era were the best team ever in hockey. Let's just look at their starting lineup: Steve Shutt, 60 goals; Jacques Lemaire, 35 goals; Guy Lafleur, 52 goals; on defence, Serge Savard, Hall of Famer; Larry

Robinson, Hall of Famer; in goal, Ken Dryden. Five out of the six starters were Hall of Famers. One year, they only lost eight games, and only one of those at home. Imagine losing only once at home. Out of the eight games lost, Boston beat them three times. We could beat them one game and leave, but in the playoffs, it was a tough go. Because of their depth, their third line could have been the first line on most clubs. We had been in two wars already, with the L.A. Kings and the Philadelphia Flyers. The L.A. series meant going back and forth across the States, and it was always a battle with the Broad Street Bullies. Meanwhile, Montreal had a picnic with the Toronto Maple Leafs. They could have walked to Toronto, so they were rested and ready to go.

Montreal and Boston players did not like each other. We had played the Canadiens and lost the last two finals, and we were determined to not make it three in a row. They had a great defence, great goalie, and four strong lines, and they had the master, Scotty Bowman, who knew all the tricks, behind the bench.

One time, he got to the rink at 8:00 A.M. when the refs were skating and he taunted them: "You won't call penalties on the Bruins"—that kind of stuff. He showed the press a video of all the penalties he thought we should have got. He sent all his players onto the ice after a goal to intimidate the other club. He knew all the tricks.

To stop this, I told my players to go on the ice after they scored. My players thought I was nuts. I explained that Scotty told *his* players to do it, so when Montreal players went out to congratulate their scorer, we jumped on, too, to congratulate our goalie. Ridiculous, I know, but Dave Newell, the ref, came over and said, "You can't do that. Forty guys milling around on the ice. There's bound to be trouble."

I must admit, it did look ridiculous. I said to Newell that if Scotty could send his guys over to congratulate the scorer, we could go on the ice to congratulate our goalie. He had to admit that there was no rule against it. I promised not to send my guys if Scotty promised not to send his. The ploy stopped. They put a rule in later that you could not send a guy onto the ice after a goal unless it was overtime.

The Bruins and I felt we were against the world and that the world was against us. I remember we were in first place in our division and had no All-Stars on the All-Star teams. We fumed at that one, but it motivated us.

The Boston GM, Harry Sinden, and I were not talking by now. We were even staying at different hotels. It was not pleasant. I knew I was gone. My days were numbered.

I still laugh at a cartoon from the *Boston Globe*. It showed Harry sitting behind his desk, and I was standing in front of the desk. Harry had a big gun in his hand. And the caption read, "Don, sit down, I want to discuss the lifetime contract I gave you."

It was not pretty. I thought one day I would be friendly. It was in the Montreal Forum, amongst a bunch of reporters. I said, "Nice shirt, Harry."

He said, "Is that right? What you're saying is the rest of my shirts are horseshit?"

I answered, "Come to think of it, you're right."

I never tried to be friendly after that, and when Harry said he didn't expect us to get past the quarter-finals, that was it.

I was making $60,000 and happy to be making the money, but the average salary for coaches in the NHL was over $100,000 (now over $1,000,000). I had won Coach of the Year and been in the Stanley Cup finals two years in a row. I was cheap labour, but coaching Boston was worth it.

I have to admit, Montreal was impressive, even in their morning skates. I remember one time, Cheevers was walking behind the glass on the way to our dressing room while Montreal was having their morning skate. I swear Steve Shutt used to fire pucks at the glass when Cheevers walked by. They knew all the tricks.

They won the first two games of that series in Montreal, and Cheevers didn't look bad, but as Randy Carlyle would say, he was okay. I knew we were not going to win with okay goaltending. People thought this was nuts. Potential Hall of Famer, but no guts, no glory, and so Gilly it was.

Scotty even poked fun about Blue picking the goalie and said he resented the fact that his dog, a beautiful German shepherd called Waldo, did not get the ink that Blue did. He said that Waldo was prettier than Blue, but I said Blue was featured in *Sports Illustrated* and therefore more famous.

I admit I went too far. I said if the series went seven games, we would be stiffed because they (meaning the NHL) wanted the glamour team, the Canadiens, in the finals, not us grinders. John Ziegler really gave it to me. He said, "I don't mind you calling us stupid, but you're calling us dishonest. I will not put up with that." (He was right, of course.)

We won the fourth game, and the Canadiens' players were in the papers, complaining about the ref. It got too hot,

and Ziegler got us all together in a little room and laid down
the law. Shut up or be fined ten thousand dollars.

We made it to game seven and we were really banged up.
A lot of guys were shot up to numb the pain before a game.
I sat in a little room by myself. I got to thinking about what
a war we'd fought to get here. Losing the first two right here
in the Forum, promising the players we would be back here
for a seventh game. Somehow I believed we would be—it
was not just a hollow promise to keep their spirits up—and
here we were. I knew it would be my last year with these
beautiful guys. I knew Harry wouldn't fire me; he'd give me
an offer I could refuse, which he did, and I *did* refuse it. I
figured if he didn't get me now, he would get me later, but
I wasn't thinking about my contract that night. I was thinking we had to go right at them. Usually, teams held back and
tried to survive the Canadiens and their blitz, just tried to
not get scored on.

We were shooting, the works. Go at 'em and get 'em on
their heels was my plan, and we did. We had a 3–1 lead. Wayne
Cashman, who had the needle before the game, got a beauty
goal and then another one, and Ricky Middleton got the
other. With only nine minutes left in the game, we led 3–1.

When I was told Bob Myers was going to ref the game, I
had an uneasy feeling. I had watched the series before
between Toronto and Montreal. The Leafs and Canadiens
were in OT and it was pretty even, both teams playing well.
All of a sudden, Bob Myers called a nothing penalty on
Tiger Williams for boarding.

(Let me explain that, at that time in hockey, refs rarely
called a penalty in the third period of a tight, important

game unless it was a flagrant penalty, when he had no choice. And you know, most players and coaches want it that way—let the players decide the game.)

When you got a penalty in OT against that Montreal team, they smelled blood. They scored and put Toronto out. Tiger came out of the penalty box and went after Myers. It took four guys to hold him back. Finally, Larry Robinson of the Habs joined in to hold Tiger back from attacking Myers. I didn't blame Tiger. It was an awful penalty, especially in OT to eliminate a team.

I had this on my mind, I'm sorry to say, the whole game. I kept saying to myself, "When is this guy going to strike?" I know it's an awful thing to admit, but it's true. And then Jean Ratelle, two-time winner of the Lady Byng Trophy, who had only twelve penalty minutes all year, got called for roughing. I remember the play like it was yesterday. It was at centre ice, and Bob Gainey ran at Jean Ratelle, and as Gainey went by, Jean pushed him in self-defence. We couldn't believe Jean Ratelle got a penalty—a Lady Byng guy. It was like Myers wanted Montreal back in the game. Guy Lafleur set up Mark Napier, and in two minutes Guy Lapointe blasted one and the game was tied.

So everybody thought the end was near, that the Montreal Canadiens would score again. The crowd could sense the next goal, but Ricky Middleton fooled them with a beauty backhander to put us ahead with only 3:59 to go.

Donnie Marcotte had orders: if Lafleur goes to the washroom, you go, too. In other words, if Lafleur is on the ice, you be there too. He did a wonderful job. I remember they both got a little nick around the eyes and went off to let the

trainer look at them. Believe it or not, they were both looking at each other like two warriors waiting to see what the
other was doing. Donnie did a super job, but still Guy was
great. Donnie, with about two minutes left in the game—
we were still up by one goal—was coming off. I turned to
him to say, "Great job, Donnie." I saw the look on his face,
and he said, "Oh no." I knew exactly what he meant. I had
set up the lines, everybody knew their job (so I thought),
but somebody had jumped over the bench out of turn.
What happened?

Scotty Bowman had Lafleur stay on for three shifts in a
row. Naturally, I had Donnie stay on, and he did his usual
great job. Donnie could skate with anybody, but the look on
his face as he stood by the door coming off was a knife in
the heart. It's ironic, I know. Good guy John D'Amico, the
linesman, saw the seventh guy right away. I can't prove it,
but I do believe he was giving us a chance to get that guy off
the ice. He didn't want a great series to be decided this way.
Unfortunately, nobody came to the bench except John D.

Honestly, folks, I can still see John looking at me with his
hand in the air, looking at me with those big brown eyes as
if to say, "Sorry, Grapes, I got to call it." What a feeling. It is
hard to describe how you actually feel. I'm lightheaded as I
write this right now.

I had to put Donnie right back on, and we were doing
okay. About a minute and a half to go in the penalty, and we
had the Cup, beating the great Canadiens right in their own
barn. New York Rangers, here we come. I saw Guy wandering up the right side, but Donnie got him. He sent the puck
to Jacques Lemaire, who was straddling the blue line—one

skate in our end and the other out—and Guy was flying. I thought Lemaire was off-side, but I never mentioned it after the game. I'm not going to be a spoilsport after a game and series like that.

Lemaire feathered a pass. I mean, it's one of those passes you dream about. It's right on the money and Guy, in full flight, slapped the puck. It skimmed along the ice about an inch above the ice for the post, just inside. Gilbert never had a chance. Terry Sawchuk couldn't have stopped that one. One-forty-three to go. I'll never forget the time. It's burned in my memory, and if I do happen to forget, people always remind me. And if people don't remind me, it's always on ESPN, CBC, NBC, etc.

Tied, we went to the dressing room. Imagine how they felt. They'd given it their best shot and were still tied. My speech was, "Lookit, when we were down 2–0 at the starts of this series, if I had said to you we'd be back here for a seventh game and we'd go into overtime and had a chance to win, would you be happy? Well, here we are, seventh game, we can beat these guys. This will show them what we're made of." They bought it and came out smoking. In fact, I remember at the start of the period, Marcotte put a pass out from behind Montreal's net and Dryden was looking behind the net. The pass was perfect, to Terry O'Reilly. He put it in the top corner and it was going in. We jumped up on the bench and Terry had his stick in the air, but Dryden was on his knees. It would have gone in on a normal goalie, but Kenny was so tall it hit the top of his shoulder and just skimmed the crossbar. They came back and Yvon Lambert put it by Gilly for the winner.

(About thirty years later, I had a conversation with Kenny

and I said, "Just thinking, Kenny, if you were not so tall, that puck would have gone in and we would have won the Cup." Kenny, with his quick wit, came back, "Ah, don't sweat it, Don. If you had won the Cup, you just would have been one of those run-of-the-mill guys who won the Stanley Cup instead of a famous guy on TV.")

Going into our dressing room after the game was the hardest thing I ever had to do. There was silence. The players just sat there, some half-undressed. I saw blood on underwear where they'd had their shots to freeze shoulders, legs, you name it. I forget what I said—something about being proud of them—and then looked at Gerry Cheevers, who had tears in his eyes. Tears came to my eyes, too. We were so close. One minute and forty-three seconds, too many men. What a way to lose the Cup.

No matter whose fault it might have been, it was really mine. I honestly believe that. I'm not just saying that. I should have realized the triple shift might confuse someone. I should have watched more closely what was going on, not telling Donnie "Nice shift."

I stood on a plastic milk carton outside the room and took the questions from the reporters. Funny—they were all in our room, not Scotty's. I knew why. It was a good, juicy story, that a coach could have too many men on at that time. They were not too cruel. One guy said, "You should have had Gilbert in earlier. If you had of had him in earlier, you might have won." I'm not too proud, but I said, "Yeah, and if my aunt had balls, she'd be my uncle." Crude—I'm sorry. I smartened up after that and took the slings and arrows. Heck, I deserved them!

It was a long flight back to Boston. The guys were going to a bar after we landed and they wanted me to go, too, but I just couldn't. When we said goodbye at the airport, I knew I wouldn't coach these beautiful players again. I knew it was "win or you're gone," and I drove home with tears in my eyes.

I had the radio on—not the news, but an FM station on with music to get my mind off the game. I know this is hard to believe, but there was a group back then called Jigsaw, and they had one big hit called "Sky High." Hearing them sing about blowing it all sky high was another knife in my heart.

I got home. Rose and Blue were waiting. Rose had tears in her eyes. Rose and I sat and had more than a few beers. Rose said it wasn't my fault. I thanked her, but I knew it was. It was getting late. Finally I said, "Rose, don't wait up. Blue and I are going for a walk. We might be gone for a long time."

✻ ✻ ✻

I gotta say, the smartest guys I met in hockey were Sam Pollock, GM of the Montreal Canadiens, and Punch Imlach. Punch was a guy who knew how to coach and knew the gut feel of hockey, and he had the Stanley Cups to prove it. But Sam was the guy who pulled strings to get the best players. For instance, did you know that Guy Lafleur should have ended up in Oakland on the California Golden Seals? They were the team that looked like they were going to finish last and get the first-overall pick in 1971, which would have been Guy Lafleur.

In May 1970, Sammy sent Ernie Hicke and the Canadiens' 1970 first-round pick to the Seals for their first-round pick in 1971. Ernie was a good player who averaged 16 goals a year over his NHL career. The Seals used the Canadiens' pick to get Chris Oddleifson, but they traded him away before he played for them. Chris was a defensive player, scoring 95 goals in 524 games, but things were not working out for Sammy. In 1970–71, the L.A. Kings went into a slump, and it looked like the California Golden Seals could end up ahead of the Kings in the standings. That would mean the Kings would get the first pick and Guy.

Sammy went to work. He sent a real good player named Ralph Backstrom to the Kings for Gord Labossiere and Ray Fortin. They never played for Montreal. Sammy just took them in the trade to help L.A. with its payroll. The Kings ended up ahead of the Seals, and Sammy had Guy.

I got to admit, Guy was okay the first three years for Montreal but did not live up to his potential. When he took off his helmet and started to fly, he was sensational. Why he took off after ditching his bonnet, I don't know. Maybe he liked his lovely long hair flying. Whatever it was, it sure worked, because that's when he became a superstar. In his first three years, he got 29 goals, 28 goals and 21 goals. The year he got rid of his helmet, he scored 53 goals, then 56, 56, 60, 52 and 50 in the next five years—never below 25. He ended up playing in 1,126 games, with 560 goals, 793 assists, 1,353 points. In the playoffs he played in 128 games, scored 58 goals, had 76 assists and 134 points. He played in six All-Star Games, won the Art Ross Trophy (scoring title) three times, the Hart Trophy (MVP) twice, Conn Smythe Trophy

(MVP in the playoffs) and the Lester Pearson Award (best player as voted by the players' association) three times.

He was always the first player in the arena, and the first guy on the ice. In fact, when I helped coach Team Canada in 1976, he and Bobby Clarke and Bobby Orr were in the dressing room at two-thirty in the afternoon for a 7:00 P.M. game. He was always ready to go.

There were many things I admired about Guy Lafleur—the way he could wire a puck in full flight, the soft hands—but I think what I admired most was the way he carried himself, something like Jean Béliveau, a gentleman. He took a lot of abuse, but he never complained, never whined to the ref, just took it and kept going.

Yes, Sam Pollock pulled off a great deal, got a superstar from the Seals for nothing, but you know what? I wish the California Golden Seals had kept their first-round pick and got Guy, if you know what I mean . . .

* * *

Earlier in the book I wrote about Albert "Babe" Siebert and his tragic end. One of his teammates on the Montreal Canadiens, Howie Morenz, also had a tragic fate. In 1950, "The Stratford Streak" was voted by the Canadian Press as the greatest star in hockey for the first half of the twentieth century. Rocket Richard got four votes. Howie Morenz had twenty-seven. When he played, he was called the Babe Ruth of hockey, won three Stanley Cups, three Hart Trophies (as the MVP of the NHL) and two Art Ross Trophies (leading scorer in the NHL).

Howie's life in hockey almost ended before it began. When he was young, he scalded his legs and they didn't know if he would walk again, let alone play. He was a sensation in his hometown of Stratford and really didn't want to go to Montreal. He wanted to stay in Stratford, but was forced to go to Montreal, where he was a sensation again. On his first shift, he scored a goal, and there was no looking back. Montreal won the Stanley Cup against Calgary in his first season as a Canadien.

Howie was of those gifted guys like Bobby Orr or Wayne Gretzky. They could read and anticipate where the puck was going. Howie was a fast fashion plate, a sharp dresser, and he was a fun guy who enjoyed life—and at times, enjoyed life a little too much. He played at full speed at all times, could shoot in full stride, not coasting before he shot, and the crowd loved him. He was the idol of the Montreal fans, but when you play that hell-bent-for-leather style, you get injured a lot. (Just ask Bobby Orr. I once asked Bobby, "Why don't you take it easy once in a while, and not take those chances?" He answered, "It's the only way I know how to play." I guess that's what made guys like Bobby and Howie great, but Bobby and Howie both paid the price.)

Montreal proved the old saying, "What have you done for me today?" and traded Howie to the worst team in the NHL, the Chicago Blackhawks. When he returned to the Forum as a Hawk, he scored and the Montreal fans give him a standing ovation.

Howie is like Bobby Orr. Bobby Orr put people in the seats of an arena. They were worth the price of admission.

The two could have the crowd on their feet when they touched the puck.

Howie scored 40 goals in 1929–30, but when you adjust the goals at that time and now, it works out to over 80 goals. And you must realize that at the time Howie played, it was more difficult to score a goal, so think if he played today. And he was a playoff guy, too. His records were unbelievable at that time.

Howie's style of play and the injuries started to pile up, but Montreal got Howie back and he was king again. The crowd still loved him, even though injuries had taken their toll and he was not the Howie of old, but still magic, till the night of January 1937, when it all ended. As usual, he broke around a big, tough defenceman, Earl Seibert, and as he went into the corner, his skate caught in a net and Earl nailed him into the boards and badly broke Howie's leg. The fans at the game said they could hear the crack all over the building.

Howie in the hospital was not a good patient. Despondent, he drank with his buddies who came to see him.

Howie somehow knew he was going to die. He sensed he would never play again and he couldn't see living without hockey. On March 8, 1937, he died in his sleep at age thirty-four; on March 12, 1937, the Montreal Forum was packed with fans there to attend the funeral of Howie and say a final farewell to its greatest star.

Hall of Famer Aurèle Joliat said it best: "Howie just loved to play hockey more than anyone ever loved anything, and when he realized that he would never play again, Howie died of a broken heart."

* * *

Back then, the Montreal Canadiens lost two star players within a couple of years of each other. Neither player was treated particularly well by the club.

The world of hockey back in those days did not take care of their own, especially the Montreal Canadiens, who should have been ashamed of the way the families of both stars were treated after their deaths. The Montreal Canadiens of the current day treat their former players better than any team in sport. "Once a Canadien, always a Canadien." Ex-players have special rooms, are treated royally, get the red-carpet treatment. When there is a reunion, they fly in the former players, everything paid for. If any are having a tough time with money, they are helped.

I am not going into the tough times of the families of Howie and Babe. There were benefit games for the stars' families that raised very little, and both families fell on hard times. That is why great men like Ted Lindsay of the Detroit Red Wings tried to get a players' association for the families. Thank the Lord this would not happen to families today. The NHL and the players' union take care of the families. The NHL is a strong association, and it was made strong by men like the Babe Ruth of hockey, who packed the stadiums everywhere in the NHL he played, on the road or at home: Howie "The Stratford Streak" Morenz.

* * *

I always feel sorry for the player who "rides the pines," as they say. I know from experience how humiliating it can be, because I did it for a whole year and the playoffs. We won the championship, so it was a tough year. Thank goodness I only did it for a year; some guys do it their entire career. I don't know how they could stand it. I know what some people say: "Well, they're getting paid." It doesn't work that way. You get up the morning of a game, have your tea and eggs, toast, go to the morning skate thinking things will change and you'll play. Maybe somebody is hurt (yes, it's like in the way when somebody is shot, you feel bad, but you're glad it's not you). After the morning skate, you go home and have your pre-game meal, have your nap, get the equipment on, warm up—and then you sit. Your family watches, you see them for the drive home. It's embarrassing, and so when I became the coach of the Rochester Americans, I vowed nobody would ride the pines for me. In Boston, all my tough guys got 20 goals. It's just not right for a guy to sit and be sent out like a mad dog.

I hurt my knee at training camp and all I did was go out and fight. I think I took it out on the guys I was fighting. I was so ticked off. The old saying, "He sat at the end of the bench"? It's not true. If you noticed, the guys who are benched are always in the *middle* of the bench, so the forwards are at one end and the defence are at the other end and you're stuck in the middle (sounds like that song, "Stuck in the middle with you"). And for some reason, the organization blames the guys who don't play. Bobby Schmautz told me a story about when he played for the Chicago Blackhawks. The Blackhawks played a lousy game and lost.

Billy Reay, the coach, came in and yelled, hollered and said, "There's going to be changes on this club."

Bobby and another guy who never played a shift were sent down the next day. For some reason, the coaches like to pick on the guy who doesn't play. I don't understand it. You would go in and say, "Why aren't I playing?" and the usual answer was, "Well, if you played better, you'd play." No sense in arguing, saying, "How can I play better if I don't play?"

I love the line of an old-time player called Kenny Doraty. The coach had him "riding the pines." The team was losing and the coach yelled at Kenny, "Doraty, you never scored a goal," and Kenny came back with a beauty: "Well, Coach, I'll tell you, it's tough scoring a goal from my angle of the bench." Isn't that great? I wish I was as quick as Kenny.

I remember the year I didn't play and sat on the bench. After one game, I packed my equipment and threw it under the bus as we were leaving on a road trip that night to Hershey. I sat in the car with Rose, complaining about not playing. Finally, she said, "I'm sick of you always complaining to me about not playing. This Joe Crozier [the coach] . . . why don't you complain to him?"

"All right, I will. Good idea," said I.

I got out of the car, grabbed my bag, went to Joe, and said, "I want to play. I'm tired of sitting on the bench." And for emphasis, I kept hitting him with my bag.

Joe said, "All right, you'll play in Hershey."

I didn't.

I remember one game in the final for the American League championship. We were getting beat 5–1 in Quebec with five minutes to go. Joe benched a regular and put me out. I know what for—to straighten a guy out. I did straighten the guy out in a beauty fight, and then we come back to Rochester for the next game. I did not play, as usual, but the game in Quebec where I had the fight had been on TV and the fans saw the fight and wanted me to play. So they started to chant, "We want Cherry! We want Cherry!" (I'm glad Crozier didn't do what the coach of the Toronto Maple Leafs, Punch Imlach, did when the fans started to chant, "We want Shack! We want Shack!" They wanted Eddie "The Entertainer" Shack to play. After a while, when the crowd kept up the "We want Shack" chant, Punch tapped Eddie on the shoulder and said, "Shack, go up and see what they want." The rest of the players killed themselves laughing at Shack.)

The crowd kept it up, even though we were winning by a big score. I kept saying to myself, "Please don't put me on. My legs are like lead."

Joe put me on with five minutes to go, I guess because of the big score, and the crowd cheered. The first shift, a guy walked around me and scored. It was, "Now you see why I don't put him on." The crowd never yelled "We want Cherry" again.

I was fortunate that my knee came around okay, and from then on in my career I took a regular shift, but my heart always goes out to the guy in the middle of the bench. That's why, if he happens to get a goal, I always highlight the goal on *Hockey Night in Canada*; I always considered they are one of the group. It's like last year in the playoffs between Montreal and the New York Rangers. I was walking out to do the opening of the first game in Montreal. Now, the opening was timed down to the last second, and we were hurrying along the hall. We wound around a corner, and there were the Black Aces of the New York Rangers (the Black Aces are the guys who aren't playing and are just there in case of injury) and they wanted a picture taken with me. The TV girl said, "We can't. We have to hurry." I told her I'd rather miss the opening than turn these guys down. They all had their cameras, and we got the pictures taken. You can't believe how good I felt that these guys wanted to have their picture taken with me. After all these years, I'm still one of the guys.

* * *

I had my disappointments when I was in Colorado, coaching the Rockies. One was the backstabbing by an ex-teammate and friend. The story goes like this. The Rockies were playing in Philly. We were staying at the Hilton hotel, which was walking distance from the Philadelphia Spectrum, which was great. Walk over to the game and back again after the game. But it was a long way from the downtown and all the bright lights. Now, we had been on the road a long time and the players were good guys. I knew they wanted to have a few beers together, and I knew if they had to pay big money for cabs to go downtown, they would stay a long time; as we had an early flight the next morning, I made the decision to let them have beer in the hotel bar.

Now, the policy of teams was for the players not to drink in the hotel bar. This was for many reasons. The GMs and scouts and newspaper guys drank in the hotel bar, with no owners. Anyway, I let the players have a few in the bar at the hotel and they were well behaved. Did you notice I said scouts drank in the hotel bar? One of our scouts was in the bar and sat with me the whole night. He was an ex-teammate and, I thought, a friend. In fact, now that I think of it, he was my defence partner in my early days; but I guess he could see the handwriting on the wall of my future with the Rockies, which was not good, and decided he didn't like me that much after all, and after sitting all night with me and the players (and me buying!), he phoned the GM and told him that the players were partying in the hotel lobby of the Hilton and I was drinking with them and the GM, who was building my coffin, phoned the owner and informed him.

I had two guys on the club called Kevin Morrison and Trevor Johansen, two defencemen who were good guys, never any trouble. After they had a few, they both had some chocolate cake, and as guys will, one guy threw a puck at the cake and the other guy threw some and some got on the floor of the hall (had I known of the cake, I would have given the housekeeper a couple hundred dollars to clean it up, no problem). The manager of the hotel phoned our GM, who was delighted to tell the owner we had a wild party in the hotel and damaged the hotel's carpeting. I had gone through the rooms to make sure everything was all right, and I think the only thing I did was straighten a lamp shade (it's funny, I can still see that room), but this was one of the many nails the GM was putting in my coffin. You know I expected that from him, but I really was disappointed in my ex-teammate turning rat.

I got fired at the end of the year, which I expected. The

My favourite picture of Luba and Blue at the cottage.

Ron is telling me I'm wrong about something.

With one of the classiest guys I know, Dick Irvin, Jr.
When Dick gets on TV, he makes us look like amateurs.

With Kathy Broderick who is the producer of "Coach's Corner"
and my Twitter person at a Heritage Game.

Getting ready to do my dance in Times Square
for *Hockey Night in Canada*.

With Arva and Doug Orr in front of the Orr family home
in Parry Sound, with my son Tim. Arva and Doug were two
beautiful people who I counted as friends.

And there's Ron telling me he's #1.

Me doing my stand-up in Afghanistan with the unhappy
US troops and Jimmy Mac.

Me entertaining the Royal 22nd in Afghanistan.
That's Defence Minister Peter MacKay in the
background (left) and Jimmy Mac (right).

With Tim at a minor hockey game. Tim scouts the minor midget for the Ontario Hockey League. One of the happiest moments of my life.

With Cindy and Bobby, and just a few of his trophies
at Bobby's golf tournament in Parry Sound.

With Ron in Sochi. What do those fingers mean?

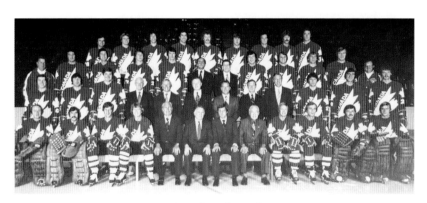

Team Canada 1976.
This is the greatest team ever put together.
We had to cut fifty goal scorers.

Christopher Lawson is a Canadian photographer working on a
portrait project of significant Canadians. He asks them to pose with
something that has great personal value. I posed with a picture of Jesus
that I have had for 65 years. It has travelled with me to 53 different cities.

team was sold two years later and went to New Jersey, and my ex-teammate who ratted lost his job and struggled to get another. The word had got out he was not to be trusted. Hockey gods or karma will always get you in the end.

* * *

I'm often asked what team I think is the best ever to play hockey. There is no doubt it's the 1976–77 Montreal Canadiens. In the 80-game regular season, the Canadiens lost only eight games all year—and just one at home. I know this is hard to believe—one game lost at home. The Boston Bruins were the Lunch Pail Gang—punch in at seven-thirty and never stop working. We beat the Canadiens the one time they lost at home, and actually beat them in three out of the five games we played against them. Like I said, we could beat them in a single game and not play them again for a month, but once they got you in the playoffs, game after game, their depth took over, and their power play was a killer. They seemed to always get the first power play. The refs would give them about three of the first four power plays, they would get up about 4–1, and then you'd get a power play. One time, I refused a penalty with a minute and a half to go because it was so obvious they were trying to even out the penalties. The ref came once and said, "If you don't send a guy on, we will give you another penalty." I said, "Go ahead. Who cares?"

Wayne Cashman, our captain, knew I was in trouble and said, "Grapes, don't let them get the shutout. Let's try to score." Good old Cash, he knew if I followed through I would be in trouble. He was trying to get me out of trouble. I said "All right, go ahead," but they really didn't need the referees. Their lineups were unbelievable.

They were tough, too—Pierre Bouchard, six-two, 240 pounds; Rick Chartraw, six feet, over 200 pounds; Robinson was six-four. They could beat you any way, and they showed no mercy when they would play a weaker club. They never let up. Scotty Bowman would not allow it. Scotty was a tough coach. The players did not really enjoy his tough ways. Steve Shutt said, "During the season, we hated Scotty. The only time we loved Scotty is when we got our playoff cheque for winning the Stanley Cup."

It was my bad luck to be coaching the Boston Bruins for five years at the time when the Canadiens were at their very best, but if you're going to be beat, at least you were beat by the very best.

* * *

I was sitting in the airplane, staring out the window, on our way to L.A. Ron was sleeping. He has that knack—one I unfortunately don't have—for sleeping on the plane. He is out cold; one time, he fell asleep as soon as we got on the plane. We went to take off and got delayed for two hours, so when we were finally ready to take off, I said to Ron, "We have landed." I set it up with the other passengers around us to let on we were landing. Ron got up, got his coat on, got out his carry-on bag and stood, ready to get off.

I wish I could sleep like that. The flights are shorter, so they tell me. I flew to London, England. Out of two hundred passengers, there was only one light turned on for the whole trip.

We are usually in a cold sweat when we finally get on the plane. With everybody having those camera phones, everybody wants a picture. Hey, I'm not complaining. When they stop taking pictures, that's when I should worry.

It's June 7. Ron has been going every day since April 8. Somehow, he hasn't worn down. I have been going every other day since April 8—not a walk in the park, but it doesn't compare to Ron's schedule. I know you're thinking, "You guys must get sick of one another." Actually, we don't spend much time together, although we live only about ten to fifteen minutes apart. I kid Ron about living in the rich Oakville area, in a house worth a couple million dollars south of the Queen Elizabeth highway, while I live north of the QEW in a middle-class area of Mississauga in a little house (which is true). Although we live close, we never see one another. He travels in different circles. He is a wine guy; I'm a beer guy who travels in no circles. Ron is really a friendly guy; he visits people, goes to dinner at restaurants, flies with Cari to islands in the South Seas, goes to Europe a lot. I, on the other hand, have never forgotten my construction ways. I don't go to restaurants, I don't visit other people, I don't fly on vacations.

I am a fortunate guy in the sense that Luba, who likes to travel, travels to different places with her family. They have a grand time together. I have always been a stay-at-home guy. I have noticed most of the coaches I know are the same way—they like to putter around in the house or go to their cottages. I have a cottage I go to; otherwise, I spend time in my basement with my TV and my three goldfish.

Ron doesn't watch TV, but I'm a TV guy. Ron reads nothing but sport books. I read books on Drake. I have every book written on Sir Francis, as well as Lawrence of Arabia, Lord Nelson, Wellington. So we are completely opposite. When I go to his room on the road, I can't believe how neat and tidy it is. He has in his bathroom: a facecloth, a towel laid out with all his toothpaste, toothbrush, etc., laid out. He has the maid in to clean up (what's to clean?). I never have the maid in, just ask for fresh towels.

I know you see us flying to L.A. and New York, and think, "Wow! They must have fun after games—dinner, bars, etc." After a game, we go back to the hotel and shower. Ron has twelve beers on ice, popcorn, peanuts, etc. We are in for the night. Occasionally after we finish, somebody will phone him, and it's "Hey Ron, we are down at Maloney's Bar. Come on over, we're having fun." He goes over, but he pays for it the next day. And of course, I keep zinging him all day, which doesn't help how he feels, but that doesn't happen too often. It's back to the hotel room for a few pops to watch the hockey or baseball game (in the playoffs) and to bed. It's the only way to survive the schedule.

I'm not complaining about life; in fact, I'm the luckiest guy in the world. Play for sixteen years (some would say "toiled" in the minors). It was a tough go and you had to be tough to survive. Guys fighting to get to the show on the way up and guys fighting on the way down. Me, I just stayed in the middle. Take care of your own injuries—the trainers were usually only equipment guys—spend days and nights on the bus. It didn't make any difference to me. I never knew any better, but it was tough on the guys from the show.

The buses were a killer to them, never having experienced a ten-hour bus trip, playing the game, getting right on the bus and another ten hours to the next game, then getting on the bus after that game and another ten hours back home for a game that night. I did it for sixteen years as a player and four more as general manager and coach. It was not an easy life for me.

I got used to it, but it's especially tough on the family. It was tough to go home after practice in Springfield when I played for the Springfield Indians. I was in the bad books for breaking my stick over the coach. I had to tell Rose we had to leave tomorrow. I'd been sent to Three Rivers, Quebec, in the middle of winter. That's when Eddie Shore gave me directions to Three Rivers "through Vermont, hit the Canadian border, turn right." We were gypsies, and I had turned into a hockey bum. I hate to admit it, but I was—no chance for the show, just surviving because I really had no trade (jackhammer specialist), no education.

I felt bad for my dad. He wanted me to make the NHL so bad, used to keep a little write up in *The Hockey News*. There wasn't much after my rookie year. I remember he kept a little part of a crossword puzzle in *The Hockey News*: "name two brothers that play for Springfield." It was Richard and myself. I felt I had let my dad down. He died at six-ty-two, and I was still slugging it out in the minors. Gosh, I wish I could have made the NHL for him so he could have been proud of me.

Ron is sleeping, like I said, on the plane and I'm staring out the window. I wonder, where did I go wrong? How—after a tremendous rookie camp, after I played my one game in the NHL and took a regular shift and was touted as a future Bruin—how did I get on the road to oblivion and the minors? It started the summer after my rookie year. Broke my shoulder playing baseball. The Bruins' manager was furious at me. I went to camp, the cut from the operation still bleeding, and went to the trainer, who gave me Band-Aids to help. Now, don't get me wrong: I blame nobody but myself for my situation. I was told not to play baseball and I did, so they had reason to be furious at me. There was no need to break my stick over Pat Egan, the coach for Springfield Indians, and sometimes I really act like a jerk. I suffered, but so did my family, and like I said, nobody to blame but myself.

But looking back, a couple of people stick out as unusually cruel, whether they knew it or not. I don't know. Hey, I had Hap Emms for a coach in Barrie. He was the toughest, meanest coach, but one of the best. He was tough on me, but that's the way he was with everybody. Eddie Shore, the Darth Vader of hockey, whose team was Devil's Island for a hockey player, was especially tough on me, but he was tough on everybody. Punch Imlach coached me. He was tough. He let Tony Schneider and me fight in practice. You could tell we were exhausted. He was tough, but again, tough on everybody.

But two guys, and what they said and did to me, keep running through my mind. And they forgot about it as soon as they did it. One person was the GM of the Boston Bruins, Lynn Patrick. He was the son of the famous hockey guy, Lester Patrick, who saved the Rangers when, in the Stanley Cup finals, his goalie got injured. He had no goalie. At forty-four years old, he went in for the goalie, won the game, and the team won the Stanley Cup. Lynn had a brother, Muzz, and they both played in the NHL, too. It was a famous hockey family. To you and most people, what he did to me will seem trivial.

I was at the Bruins camp in Boston. It was my third year. The management still hadn't forgiven me for playing baseball and getting hurt. In those days, once you were in the doghouse, you stayed in the doghouse. Guys who didn't get the ice time I was getting were called up to the show, but not me. But that's the way it was. No use crying over it; you accepted it or you quit. I was walking to practice through the Boston Garden by myself, and I saw Lynn Patrick, the GM; Milt Schmidt, the coach; and another guy I don't remember. As I walked by, Lynn Patrick said, "Don, you were on that Memorial Cup team in Barrie. What was the year?" Hey, he was talking to me. I was thrilled. As I went to answer, he said, "Ah! He wouldn't know."

It tell ya, it was like a knife in the heart. I was so embarrassed and hurt. I know it seems like nothing, and of all the bad, hurtful things that have happened to me, that was one of the killers. But the one that I remember to this day was the shot I took from a Bruin defenceman named Bill Quackenbush. I was really having a hard time with my shoulder, and like I have said, I could not shoot the puck hard. I remember it like it was yesterday. Bill really didn't have to worry about me taking his place—he was an all-star, but I must admit, a soft all-star. Put it this way: he got no penalties all year and he was a defenceman, so you can see what kind of a person he was. Still, he was an NHL player and I respected him. I took a shot at the goaltender (it was not good), and Bill turned to the coach, Milt Schmidt, and said, "Hey Milt, this guy's got a worse shot than me."

I know it doesn't sound like much, but between my shoulder, Lynn saying "he wouldn't know," and my failure to make the show, it was the final zing. I didn't say anything—what could I say? He was right, but afterward, I thought, "What kind of a man would ridicule to the coach a young player who obviously was having a bad time?"

I just thought of something. When I was a rookie hot shot in the Boston camp, I sat beside an older defenceman called Andy Branigan. Andy was near the end of his career. He told me a strange story about when he played for the New York Americans in the old NHL. Their goalie got hurt, so their coach, Red Dutton, put Andy in net, because Red knew Andy played net in lacrosse. They lost the game to Detroit 5–4, but Andy never let in a goal. Andy scored in that game before he went in net, so he scored a goal and played goal in the same game (the goalie he replaced, Andy told me, was Hall of Famer Chuck Rayner). Andy only played a few games in the NHL. The war came and he enlisted in the Royal Canadian Air Force in 1942. Andy had a tough time to make the NHL when he came back. He had given up his career to help his country, like a lot of guys who gave up their careers with the NHL.

One, for instance, Doug Orr, the dad of Bobby Orr—they tell me he was a better skater than Bobby and would have shone in the NHL, but he gave it up to enlist in the Canadian Navy. He was posted to a corvettes, guarding convoys in the North Atlantic from the German submarines. Doug gave up a career in the NHL, like Andy. It was his duty. (By the way, the corvette ships were said to be one of the most uncomfortable boats in the navy. They were called "tin cans," but they did the job.) Doug spent four years on the "tin cans," and when he got discharged, he, like Andy, found his career in the NHL gone. Both were heroes of mine.

But at the time, I just knew Andy as an old American Hockey League player near the end of his career, and it looked like I was going to take his spot (which I eventually did), but Andy (a Winnipeg boy) was so kind to me, giving me advice in hockey and life. He told me one day, after I got cut in practice, to rub cocoa butter on my cuts and they would disappear. I did, and they did disappear. I was young and single and I was staying out late, having a good time with girls. One day, Andy sat me down and said, "Don, I have found in my life you have to make a decision. You can drink or you can go out with girls, but you can't do both, because when you drink, you go home and go to bed at a reasonable hour. But if you drink and stay up late with girls, it will be the end of you. You can't do both. Make a decision." I took Andy's advice and just drank.

I think now of Hall of Famer Bill Quackenbush—famous guy, all-star, ridiculing a rookie who was hurt—and how cruel he was. It's funny, he won the Lady Byng. Andy was a confirmed minor leaguer, played fifteen years in the AHL and then went to the Eastern Hockey League. Bill Quackenbush went a whole year with no penalties, yet he was a mean man. Andy was a tough defenceman who was an enforcer type. One was soft, yet cruel; the other was tough, yet kind. Andy taught me a valuable lesson: it doesn't cost anything to be kind. It's funny; I only knew Andy for a little while at training camp—one week. Andy left after training camp—no goodbyes or anything. I never knew where he went or ever saw him again, yet I've never forgotten him and his kindness. A ship that passes in the night.

I know I have spent a lot of time on a minor leaguer who I only knew for a week, but guys like him and Doug Orr made a deep impression on me.

✻ ✻ ✻

When the experts of sports get together, one of their topics is "How great is a record?" The record the experts bring up as the greatest that was ever set is Babe Ruth's 60 home runs in 1927. But before that, in 1920, he hit 54 home runs, and the experts point to the player who hit the second-most home runs that year, George Sisler, who hit 19. Now *that* is a record. If the guy who came in second had hit 40 home runs (like in 1927, when Lou Gehrig hit 47), then Babe's record would have been good, but to hit 54 and the next guy is so far behind—that's the way they judge a record.

In Bobby Orr's third season, 1968–69, he scored 64 points—a record for a defenceman. He broke the record of 59, set by veteran defenceman Pierre Pilote, who played for the Chicago Blackhawks, in 1964–65. Pierre was a super defenceman. I remember when I broke into junior with Barrie, I carried the puck up the centre of the ice with my head down. Pierre, who played for the St. Catharines TeePees, nailed me good with a shoulder check. I saw stars for a while. I definitely would have been put in the quiet room if it happened today.

Pierre won the Stanley Cup and was voted the best defenceman three times, but Bobby came along and broke his record. And a couple years later, in 1970–71, Bobby set the record that stands today: 139 points. Imagine, the record was set at 59 points. Seven years later, Bobby scores 139. Just like Babe Ruth.

More on Bobby. As I write this, I see it's possible that a defenceman could win the Norris Trophy (for best defenceman) and be a minus hockey player. Believe it or not, three defencemen won the Norris and were minus defencemen (Randy Carlyle, minus-16 in 1980–81, Rob Blake, minus-3 in 1997–98, and Nicklas Lidstrom, minus-2 in 2010–11). When Bobby played for me in 1974–75, he scored 46 goals and had 89 assists and was a plus-123. In 1970–71, he set the all-time record: plus-123. He won the Norris eight years in a row, another record. I remember what Harry Howell said when he won the Norris Trophy in 1966–67, just before Bobby started his run. He said, "I'm glad I won this trophy this year, because with Bobby Orr around, nobody else is going to win it for a long time."

Bobby's trophies are another record nobody gets close to, starting with two Stanley Cups, eight Norris Trophies, two Hart Trophies (most valuable player), two Art Ross Trophies (leading the NHL in points), a Conn Smythe Trophy (MVP in the playoffs), MVP of the Canada Cup in 1976. Actually, 1974–75 was really his last year. Like I said, he won the scoring title (for the second time); 46 goals, 89 assists; plus-123; Norris Trophy for the eighth time. But in '76 he went to the

Canada Cup, where Canada won, with a defence that consisted of Larry Robinson, Denis Potvin, Serge Savard, Guy Lapointe and Bobby Orr. Bobby got picked as the MVP of the tournament, and really, that was his last hurrah, as they say. He left Boston on the advice of his agent and friend, Alan Eagleson. Unknown to Bobby, Boston had offered him not only a good salary but part of the Boston Bruins. Eagleson failed to inform Bobby, because he had a deal cooking with Chicago.

Bobby had to retire because of his knees. People never saw Bobby on the downside of his career, only at the top, but it was a tough pill to swallow, retiring at twenty-eight, just when defencemen are normally coming into their prime. I could go on about Bobby, but you might think I'm prejudiced because he is a friend. Let's see what the bible of hockey books says about Bobby. It's called *Players: The Ultimate A–Z Guide to Everyone Who Has Ever Played in the NHL*, by Andrew Podnieks. The book contains more than 5,600 entries. It starts the story of Bobby like this: "Perhaps on one of the cold planets out there in the vast universe there exists a player who was as good as Bobby Orr, but on this planet no man who ever put on a pair of skates can even pretend to be equal to Bobby Orr." The write-up ends: "Almost from the day he started playing in the NHL, he has inspired future players to emulate his style. There will never, ever, be another Bobby Orr."

I can't count the times I've heard a coach holler at a defenceman who screws up while carrying the puck: "Pass the puck. Who do you think you are? Bobby Orr?"

* * *

Recently, Bobby Orr was on his book tour and he was being interviewed by someone on some obscure station I never heard of. He never knew I would see it—Luba found it on the Internet. The commentator, who I'm sure never heard of me, asks Bobby, "If you were in the war and you wanted one guy you could trust by your side, who would that be?"

Bobby answered, "Oh, Grapes for sure. He would never throw me out of the foxhole."

I got all choked up. Bobby does not know I saw the interview. He won't know till he reads this book. I can tell you now, it's the greatest compliment I ever got in my life.

* * *

I remember looking at the 1976 Canada Cup team and saying, "This is the greatest team in history. We are going to have to work hard to screw this up." And you know, we almost did.

I was with the Boston Bruins—just made coach of the year in the NHL. I got a call from the head guy, Alan Eagleson, asking if I would coach along with Scotty Bowman. I said I'd love to, but I had to ask my GM, Harry Sinden. Harry was not too happy, but said okay. I remember his last words: "Don't you pick pucks out of the net for anybody."

After I told Eagleson I would do it, I asked who was coming. Eagleson started to name the guys: Rogie Vachon, Gerry Cheevers, Glenn Resch, Bobby Orr, Denis Potvin,

Serge Savard, Guy Lapointe, Bobby Clarke, Darryl Sittler, Marcel Dionne, Lanny McDonald, Paul Shmyr, Dave Burrows, Peter Mahovlich, Reggie Leach, Phil Esposito, Rick Martin, Bob Gainey, Bobby Hull, Gil Perreault, Dan Bouchard, Dan Maloney, Billy Barber, Danny Gare, Carol Vadnais, Jean Pronovost and Jim Watson. Coaches Scotty Bowman, Al MacNeil, Bobby Kromm and me. Management: Al Eagleson, Jean Béliveau, Toe Blake, Keith Allen, Sam Pollock. Doctor Doug Kinnear. Trainers Lefty Wilson and Eddie Palchak.

I said, "What a team. You know, of course, we are going to have to cut some 50-goal scorers. This is the greatest team ever." Eagleson said, "Yeah, I know. We better not screw up. We got pressure after that '72 series."

"Don't worry, Eagle, we will make it. What can stop us?" Little did I know.

We all met in Montreal and stayed at the Queen Elizabeth Hotel. We had our meeting—Eagleson, Bowman, Kromm, MacNeil, Beliveau, Blake, Allen and the head guy, Sammy Pollock. We went over everything. Sounds good, ready to go. As we were leaving, Eagleson said, "The guys go for their testing tomorrow morning."

Don: "What do you mean, 'testing'?"

Eagleson: "To see if they're in shape."

Don: "What's the test?"

Eagleson: "Bikes . . . skating, of course . . . sit-ups, push-ups . . ."

Don: "Hold it, Eagle. Have you told these guys to prepare for this?"

Eagleson: "We told them to be in shape."

Don: "But you know these guys. They have never done push-ups, chin-ups, bikes . . ."

Eagleson: "This is a brand new way of seeing if guys are in shape."

Don: "What if Potvin, Savard, Orr and Lafleur aren't in shape for the bikes? You gonna send them home?"

Eagleson: "Quit causing trouble the first day. It's done and that's it."

I was on the outs and the camp hadn't even started.

The next day at ten o'clock, I went into the exercise room and some gung-ho young college guys and gals were explaining what Lafleur—who never in his life lifted weights or rode bikes—and Bobby Hull, whose body was natural and the best of these superstars, were expected to do. They were looking at me as if to say, "Is this for real?"

Push-ups, bikes, sit-ups. This was the killer. Well, you guessed it, players pulled groins and suffered injuries. Worst of all, Bobby Hull pulled his groin. Bobby really wanted to shine. The reason Bobby, maybe the greatest left winger of all time, was left off the '72 team was because he'd signed with the World Hockey Association. There were still bad feelings about Bobby because he was the first guy to sign with Winnipeg Jets of the WHA and opened the doors for players to make big money, not only in the WHA but in the NHL too. So they kept him off the '72 team, but he was here for the '76 series. He was anxious to show his stuff, and here he was, injured because of ridiculous sit-ups.

Let me describe to you what was going on. Say you have a superstar doing sit-ups beside another superstar. They are not going to quit and look bad, so they would strain themselves. And, seeing as they were not prepared for these exercises, they hurt themselves. A lot of them came to me with their woes. I said, "Look, tell the guys to go along with this bullshit. Don't overdo it. Don't hurt yourself. So they played the game of pretending.

I thought everything was hunky-dory till one morning, when I was called to a meeting at the Forum. The brass were all there, looking glum.

"They are sending Guy Lapointe home. I know he is one of your favourites. We don't want an argument."

Don: "What has Lapointe done to be sent home in the middle of camp?"

"He refuses to run." Every morning, the college guys were making the players run a couple of miles on a track.

Don: "Now, let me get this straight: you're gonna send home one of the top defencemen in the world home because he won't run."

"That's right!"

Don: "Wait a minute, guys, we got the greatest defence pairs of all time and you're gonna break them up because he won't run."

"That's right. Please, we don't want an argument."

Don: "But guys, he works with Savard and Robinson so well. The Big Three, and then with Potvin and Orr, it's a dream."

"If we let him away with it, we will look bad and that there's no discipline."

I had to come up with something, so I said, "Guys, the reason he won't run is that he can't. He's got flat feet, and you know you can't run with flat feet. You just can't send him home." They bought it.

I happened to mention to one of the players that it was too bad Guy couldn't run because of his flat feet. They caught on.

That was my first introduction to this mentality about training.

They have the same ridiculous nonsense going on now for the young draftees in the NHL. It's called the combine. The young players come to a camp with NHL scouts who put them through that nonsense: bikes, jumping high and jumping far. (I remember the German player, Uwe Krupp, who scored the Stanley Cup winner for Colorado in 1996. The next spring, they did these tests, like the one where you see how far you can jump. Uwe tried to see how high he could jump, and came down hard on his knee. That injury stayed with him.)

The reason they say they do the testing at training camp is that when you take the test at Christmas, you will see if you have progressed. Oh, I get it: if you are a 25-goal scorer at Christmas and you take the test and you haven't progressed, are they going to send you to the minors? If a guy is scoring for me, I'm not going to worry him about testing. In fact, you could throw him off, confronting him with his test result. It's nonsense. The players know it, but they're not going public and saying it, so they play the game. What are they going to do? When I hear scouts say, "Well, there is no harm in it," I think of Uwe Krupp.

* * *

Larry Zeidel, my roommate in Hershey for two years, was one of the few Jewish players to play hockey in professional hockey. His nickname was "The Rock," and the name suited him well. He was with Detroit when they won the Stanley Cup in 1951–52. He went to Chicago and then to the minors—with me as a defence partner in Hershey of the American League. I remember I was just a kid, and he was so serious about things. One day, he said we should be like football quarterbacks. We should call out numbers for plays. Like, when I get to the back of the net, I'd call different numbers for different plays. It lasted one period. Nobody fooled with Larry and his ideas, which were far out. One day, the trainer, Scotty Alexander, made faces behind Larry's back as if he was nuts. Larry turned around and caught him, and knocked him flying. Don't fool with the Rock.

Larry always told me he would make it back to the NHL. After thirteen years, when he was almost forty years old, he told me, "Expansion is coming. I'm going to send out my resumé to make a comeback." I thought to myself, "Fat chance," but Larry fooled me. The Philly Flyers gave him a chance and he was back in the NHL at forty years old.

In 1968, when he was playing for Philly, the wind lifted the roof off the Spectrum and the Flyers had to play against Boston at Maple Leaf Gardens in Toronto. Eddie Shack and Larry got into a beauty stick fight. Both got cut. It was a sight to see. Both got suspended by Clarence Campbell.

Larry was always playing the stock markets, and when the Flyers tried to send him to the minors, Larry said he'd had enough of the minors. He retired and became a successful stockbroker.

He died June 17, 2014. It's hard to believe The Rock is gone. Somehow, it always seemed to me that Larry would be around forever. It makes me think.

* * *

I am writing this after the sixth game of the Western Conference finals between the L.A. Kings and the Chicago Blackhawks. I should say "war" instead of game: they are wearing each other out—over ninety hits between the two teams. L.A. had more hits than the two teams in the Eastern final, the Montreal Canadiens and New York Rangers, combined. Between the Rangers and Canadiens, there was a total of thirty-five hits. LA had forty-eight.

This playoff reminds me of the playoffs we used to have between the Boston Bruins and the Montreal Canadiens. In 1976 and '77, Boston ended up in a dogfight with the L.A. Kings. L.A. had a big, tough team with tons of talent and Rogie Vachon in net. Naturally, the series went seven games in 1976 and six games the year after. We would have to fly coast to coast, and the Bruins were cheap. We would fly commercial while other teams had a charter.

It was funny; before I came to the Bruins, they chartered everywhere. After my first year, Jeremy Jacobs, the owner, decided we would fly commercial. Little did he know he'd done me a favour. When we flew on a charter, we would fly back to Boston right after a game and the players would go their separate ways: some home, some to one bar, some to another bar or restaurant. When the owners, in their cheap wisdom, decided to make us go commercial, we usually had to stay overnight in the visiting city. Say it was Chicago. After the game, the whole team would go together to their favourite bar and be a team. It was so much fun. We had a family feeling. Naturally, I would be there. I did something that was never done before or since: I used to be able to go out with the players for a few pops. I know it is not a good policy, but it worked. I could do it. I would stay for a few hours, and then we had no trouble.

If a player was traded to the Bruins, the captain, Wayne Cashman, and a few of the tough guys on the club had a meeting with the new guy and explained the rules. "We have a first-place club, no team in sports has more fun than we do, and you're not going to ruin it here or break rules. There's not many, but they have to be followed. We've never been fined or suspended. If you break the rules, you're gone. If you have a few pints the night before the game, you can get a little glow, but don't stay out the night before a game. A few guys have broken this rule. They were sent to the minors or gone, traded the next day.

"Next, don't get into trouble in the hotel where we are staying. If you do, the hotel manager will phone the GM of the Bruins, Harry Sinden, and now we're all in trouble. Next, don't get arrested. We have a beautiful thing here. Sometimes it's hard for me not to smile at the wife when we go on the road. I can hardly wait to get on the road to have fun. For instance, win or lose, after a game, Grapes will say, 'The bus leaves at ten o'clock for the airport. In other words, go out and have fun, but be ready to leave at ten o'clock.'

"So we have three rules off the ice. Naturally, we have to

look sharp travelling, so don't screw up and make Grapes look bad, because if you do, you'll hear from us."

I used to let the veterans run the dressing room. If it came down to trouble, I would take care of it. I was one of them. It was us against the world; if I saw a slight, I would make a big deal of it. I used to say, "We're a first-place club, and look: no votes for all-star." Stuff like that.

We were like a band of brothers, and the winning and fun never stopped, even in the practices. The practices were not long—an hour and ten minutes—but always moving. No stoppages for a blackboard talk, and instructions were given before going on the ice. There is nothing worse than working up a sweat and having a coach make you stop and have him draw plays on a blackboard like you're at public school. (The best coach in junior hockey, Brian Kilrea, never used a blackboard. He would not have them in the dressing room.) My practices were like clockwork, always the same. You are thinking "boring." Never. Fast and furious, like a hockey game. Nobody yawned in my practices. They were a hockey player's practices.

I knew the cheaters, and they paid the price after practice. One time, when I was in the American Hockey League as coach and general manager of the Rochester Americans, one guy stayed out late and did what I call cheating the hockey club. I made him skate so hard after practice, all by himself, with me yelling "again," and while he was lying on the ice, gasping for breath, one of the cleaning ladies who was sweeping the empty arena came down and said, "Stop what you're doing to that poor man. That's inhumane." I was almost finished with the punishment, so I said to her, "You're right, ma'am. I'll stop right now."

The Rochester Americans, the Boston Bruins, the Colorado Rockies all had fun when I coached. Mike Milbury, who played for me and is now a TV commentator on NBC, when asked what kind of a coach I was, said, "I never had so much fun as I did playing for Grapes. He was a great coach." Because if you have a job and it's fun and you look forward to going to work, you'll do a better job. I would call an optional practice and everybody would show up. I had to tell the vets to stay home.

I mentioned earlier that I went with the idea that everybody was against us. We had no friends. We had to look after ourselves, and the players had to feel that I would lay my job on the line for them. For instance, when we would have an injury, I would tell Harry Sinden, the GM, I didn't want a replacement. We would go a man short. He was not happy, but seeing as we always won, he'd go along with it. It sounds like I'm taking a chance—not at all. I knew the players could see what I was doing, protecting their jobs. They thought I was taking a chance for them. In a way, I was, but you really don't need eighteen players. It's a joke to have that many players. The players learned it when they got more ice time, and between getting more ice time and thinking I'm protecting their jobs, they went 1,000 per cent.

I know what you're thinking: "If you don't need eighteen players and the players like more ice time, why have eighteen players?" The player's union would not put up with anything less than eighteen players.

I changed after my first year with the Bruins. The first year, I come from Rochester, a minor leaguer—coach of the year in Rochester, but still a minor leaguer. The Bruins were Stanley Cup champs in 1972 and went to the finals with Philly in 1974, the year before I arrived. I did not act like I did with Rochester. I thought, "They'll be there when the bell rings." My first year, we were in the playoffs against Chicago. In the deciding game, we outshot Chicago 52–18 and lost.

Tony Esposito was a great goalie. We beat him in the first game, 8–2. The papers said he was finished. When I read that about Tony, I knew we were in trouble. Sure enough, he stood on his head and you couldn't put a pea by him, and we lost.

I had a meeting with the GM, Harry Sinden. I said, "Look, Harry, I let you down. If you want to let me go, I won't demand the last two years of my contract." Harry was great. He said, "Don't be silly. But coach like you did in Rochester." But then Harry said the fatal words: "Look, we have to win. If you don't, we're both gone. Do anything. Make me the heavy, just win."

I went home that night and played that song by The Who, "Won't Get Fooled Again," and did an about-face. I made enemies with the NHL, the Bruins organization, scouts and, I'm ashamed to say, the guy who took me from the minors and gave me a chance: Harry. I showed no mercy. If I was going, I was going. The team actually thought the league, the organization, everybody was against them, and it worked. Four first-place finishes, twice to the finals and twice more to the semifinals. Winning percentage: .658. Coach of the year. I wasn't making much money, but I was having fun. I loved the players and they loved me. Fun, winning . . . who could ask for anything more?

But all good things must come to an end. Harry and Paul Mooney, the team president who represented the owner, Jeremy Jacobs, had had enough of the bad-guy routine. Yeah, we won, and they made money, but I was becoming unbearable. The players would only listen to me. I remember one time, Brad Park, our star defenceman, and two other regulars had played in eight exhibition games and did not have to play any more. The Bruins organization had scheduled a big-time exhibition game in Montreal at the Forum. It sold out. Top prices for an exhibition game. Now, going to Montreal, you had to have your players play. It was big time. The players told the Bruins, "No, we have played eight games. We're not playing." What to do?

The organization had to come to me and say, "You talk them into playing. They'll do anything for you. If you don't, we are in trouble." I went to the players and said, "Look, play the game. They'll owe us a favour. I'll get them to pick up the tab for the beer after the games on the road." They played.

But it had to end. I was beginning to act like it was my team, like I owned the club. In other words, I got carried away with myself, so Harry and Paul Mooney had a meeting with me, and over lunch they said, "Look, Don, we appreciate the wins and the way the team plays. But you've got to change—especially your relationship with the press." The press and I had a love affair going. If they missed a column, they could phone me at 11:00 P.M. and I'd give them a column. I helped them and they protected me. For instance, after some games, I'd go nuts, yelling at the league, Harry, Paul Mooney and the refs, and I'd wake up in the morning, thinking, "Oh, why did I say that? I'm done." But I'd pick up the paper and they'd have written what I'd said as if it was their own idea. The Boston press was so good. They figured I helped them, so they'd protect me. It was beautiful. But Harry and Paul Mooney had had enough, and so this was the rule from now on: you change, or see you later.

I said to Paul and Harry, "Look, I could say I will change, but you and I know eventually I will say something." In my heart, I knew I was done. The only reason they didn't fire me was because I was so popular. I made it easy for them. In other words, if they didn't get me now, they would get me later, so we parted, shook hands and it was friendly.

The players all came to the house that night and so did the press. The players and the press were as sad as I was, and so was Blue, who sat beside me the whole time. It's funny how dogs know what's going on. So it was sad, but there were no hard feelings. These things happen.

But something happened the next day. The Bruins had a day for the fans, and a friend of mine—not a good friend, but a friend—told me Harry said to him, "I wonder what Blue thinks now?" Meaning I used to say, "Blue says we should play Cheevers tonight." It was sort of a running joke with the press. That did it. The feud started, and it lasted for years, Harry and me sniping at one another, me on "Coach's Corner" and him in the Boston press.

I had an unfair advantage with *Hockey Night in Canada*.

My son, Tim, and I were driving to see a minor midget game one night and he said, "You know, Dad, you've known Harry all your life. Playing against him. He gave you your very first NHL chance. Why don't you bury the hatchet?" And I thought, "Tim is right." So I extended the olive branch to Harry. I went on "Coach's Corner" and said something like "Harry Sinden is the best general manager in hockey. I was lucky he was my GM." Somebody told Harry, and he came back with, "Oh yeah? Well, if a guy like Sam Pollock said it, it would mean something." The feud was back on with a vengeance.

Till one day, I got invited to the closing of the Boston Garden. It was called "The Last Hurrah." The Bruins had all the players and coaches from the past. (They gave the players sweaters, jackets and caps, and they gave the former coaches beautiful jackets, shirts and sweaters. I loved a Boston Bruins jacket.) We really were treated royally. Unfortunately for me, I did all kinds of interviews on TV, and when I got back to the dressing room where we'd all met, somebody (one of the former players) had taken all my stuff. I ended up without even a program. But at least the Bruins and I made up after all these years. Ron MacLean still kids me that Harry and I hugged on the ice—I'm not the hugging kind.

I especially liked it when Harry took me around and introduced me to all the former coaches and players. He introduced me to Pat Egan, who was my coach in Springfield (and who, along with Eddie Shore, made my life miserable in Springfield). Pat was the guy who was delighted to send me to Three Rivers, Quebec, at Christmastime. I have to admit, it made my heart feel good.

Harry: "You know Pat Egan, don't you, Don?"

I thought of a million things to stay, but I chickened out and just said, "Yeah, I know Pat."

The reason I started to write this story was to talk about how hard it is to be like the L.A. Kings, with all the travel and playing three series that went the full seven games and how hard they hit. In the sixth game of their series with Chicago, the Kings had 48 hits and Chicago had 35. It was a war. Chicago played well, but lost the series in a heartbreaker.

I am writing this the morning after the seventh game, which L.A. won in overtime with Alec Martinez scoring the winner on a shot from the point. I leave tomorrow for L.A. I predict the Kings will win the Stanley Cup in six games. I will leave this on my desk and pick up the end of the story when I come back from the Stanley Cup. L.A. in six.

Yeah, I know I was wrong. L.A. won it in five games. My kind of team: big, tough, and fifteen Canadians.

HOCKEY TODAY

ONE NIGHT ON "COACH'S CORNER," I showed some basketball players walking into their game dressed like slugs, and then I showed some hockey players walking into their game dressed like they just stepped out of *Esquire*, and then I showed Evander Kane of the Winnipeg Jets in an interview, and he looked like a male model. I was making a point. Hockey players have respect for themselves and respect for the game. In many ways—the way they act and the way they dress. Football, baseball and basketball have many suspensions for drugs and for violent acts with knives, guns, you name it. Of course, when you have seven hundred hockey players, you are going to have some jerks, but they are few and far between.

The NHL has a strict drug policy. They do not give a slap on the wrist for drug use like other sports do. If you take drugs in the NHL, you might as well put a big *D* on your forehead. It is never forgotten and never forgiven, and surprisingly, it is not forgotten by the other players.

When I coached the Bruins, a young player got caught

with marijuana when he was on a road trip with his team and got caught at customs coming into Canada. He had left a joint in the pocket of a shirt and forgotten about it. Headlines in the papers and he was suspended. He was never the same. "Hey, isn't that the guy that got caught with the joints?" I was surprised to hear the Bruins hollering from the bench to the players: "Hey Pothead," they shouted, because the players are all tarred with the same brush if one gets caught. I know what you're thinking. They were mad at him for getting caught. No way. They were ticked because he made the sport look bad.

The NHL has a strict policy. Random testing on and off-season. Nobody knows when the drug teams will show up, and if you're caught, there's no mercy. It's not just a suspension; it could be your life—which is the way it should be, not like one sport where the player had in his contract that if he gets caught with drugs, he still gets paid, and when he comes back to the team, all is forgiven.

I remember back in the seventies when I coached the Boston Bruins, a player got caught with a joint. The New York Rangers management, including their coach, said they were backing our player. I had a meeting with the Bruins players. I started the meeting by saying, "You like the way the New York Rangers management and coach back their players?" Naturally, they all said yes. I said, "Well, don't expect that from me. If one of you guys gets caught with drugs, I'll cut your heart out. I not only will ruin your hockey life, I'll make it so you have no life when you go back to Canada, and don't come begging for mercy. You'll get none." Needless to say, we had no problems with drugs.

I remember a young hockey player who was a good player, who had a tough time getting drafted because he got caught with a joint. So it's the fear of getting a bad reputation. We do not treat drugs like other sports do, but I feel there is another reason. I feel it starts at a young age. In Canada, I feel we have respect for our sport. My son, Tim, works for the Ontario Hockey League and he rates the players in the Greater Toronto Hockey League to be drafted by the OHL. At nine-thirty at night, when Tim and I go out to watch the minor midget games, as we are coming into the arena, the bantams are just leaving after their game. It does my heart good to see them with their team jackets and their shirts and ties. What sport in the world has young players wearing shirts and ties to and from their games? The same as our junior teams—90 per cent shirts and ties.

I remember in the American Hockey League, we'd travel ten hours on the bus, but when we'd get off we would have shirts and ties, respect for the game and respect for ourselves.

Hockey players have a great reputation, especially down in the States, for courtesy and politeness. Bob Verdi, the great *Chicago Tribune* newspaper sportswriter, said to me once, "After the baseball players, football players, and basketball players, having the hockey players come to town is like a breath of fresh air."

There is always an exception to this policy—for instance, the colourful Derek Sanderson of the Boston Bruins, who couldn't stand wearing ties. One day, the Bruins were going on a road trip, and as they boarded the bus to the airport, Derek got on the bus without a tie. The coach, Harry Sinden, stopped him and said, "You know there is a hundred-dollar fine for not wearing a tie on a road trip. Here, take one of my ties." Derek looks at the tie of Harry's. He tosses the tie back to Harry and says, "I'll pay the hundred-dollar fine."

✳ ✳ ✳

I was sitting with a few friends, having a couple and shooting the breeze about hockey. One guy said to me, "Grapes, you've been around hockey a long time, been a lot of places. First, tell us the places you've played and coached, and what do you think you've contributed to hockey?"

I said, "It's funny you have asked where I've been playing and coaching. Stanley, our stats guy, for *Hockey Night in Canada*, once heard me say on a broadcast, 'Nobody has played or coached in as many cities as I have. I played in every professional league that existed—American Hockey League, Western Hockey League, the Eastern Professional Hockey League, and one game in the NHL. I coached in the NHL and the AHL.' Stanley handed me a list of where I played and coached. The list includes fifty-three cities I coached or played in, twenty-two different states and six different provinces. I know in a way that sounds impressive, but think about how my family had to travel to be in those leagues. I put it down to a lot of teams wanted me."

My contribution to hockey, of course, that everyone in the minors knows or should know, is how to keep the beer cold after the game on the bus. The routine: take a pillowcase from the hotel. When the bus gets rolling, put four beers in the pillowcase and hang it out the window on a freezing-cold night. In ten minutes, presto, ice-cold pops. I almost got into the AHL Hall of Fame for that one.

My other contribution to hockey, not many people know about. It's how to get an advantage in a fight. It's the old saying, "All's fair in love and war." And, I might add, in a fight. Fighting in hockey is a tough role, and any advantage you can get, you try. I always got my elbow pad off my right arm—you can't believe the difference it makes. I discovered it by accident. When I played, I had to work in the summer because we did not make much money and the kids had to eat. I developed big arms by working with a 150-pound jack-hammer all summer. The elbow pads would cut into my arms, so I cut them to loosen them up. One time, I cut too much, and when I had a fight, the elbow pads flew off. It was like my arm was free and it felt great, and I could throw twice as many punches, so from then on, I cut the right elbow pad a little more to take advantage in the fight.

If you have noticed in today's fights, the real fighters always get their elbow pads off for swinging—even the goal-ies are into it. Remember last year, Jonathan Bernier went at Ryan Miller. He cleaned Miller's clock. How, you ask? Bernier got his right arm free from his pads and was swinging free and beauty.

I remember a lot of people wondered how Félix Potvin, a little guy, did such a number on Ronnie Hextall, who was a big guy who could throw them. Same thing: Félix got his right arm out of the pads, and boy, did he go.

Now, the next trick to take advantage of your guy is one you're going to have to bear with me on. It gets a little com-plicated, so pay attention.

All hockey players wear garter belts (yes, they do, ladies) to hold their socks up. There is that little piece of rubber that sticks up on the garter belt that goes around the wire on the belt to hold the socks up. Well, sometimes that little piece of rubber breaks off. In the minors you make do, so we would substitute a dime in place of that little piece of rubber that broke off. It works perfect. What's this got to do with fighting? Patience, I will tell you.

I found when I was with a team that had big sweaters, I would get my sweater pulled over my head, which was an awful feeling as the guy rings a few on your melon. You don't have a chance. Some guys would stop, but most wouldn't, and by the time the linesman got in, you'd took quite a few. (In Rochester, I had a small sweater, so it was hard for a guy to grab, and naturally, it was hard to get the sweater over my head.) When you had a large sweater, it was easy to get the sweater over the head, so I figured, if that trick with the garter belt worked, why can't I do the same with my sweater?

So here's what I did: I got an old skate lace cut about two feet long, took one end and tied it to the button in the back that held the braces that held up your pants. Then I took a quarter and put it on the inside of the sweater in the back, wrapped the sweater around the quarter, and then I took the lace and tied it around the sweater and the quarter. Presto! The first tied-down sweater in hockey. It was now impossible to pull the sweater over my head. Brilliant, eh?

Yes, there were a lot of little tricks. Always put a lot of Vaseline all over your face to soften the blows. Another smart one was with the sweater again. When, in a fight, you see the player pulling and tugging on the sweater, it was tough on the neck. I would actually be cut on the back of my neck from the rayon sweater, and I would always have a stiff neck the next day. The trainers weren't too happy about this. But I took some scissors and cut about four inches at the back of the sweater at the neck, and then I would sew up the sweater lightly so, in a fight, it would tear away and save my neck. I never had a stiff or cut neck after that.

So there you have it, folks, some of my biggest contributions to hockey are how to keep the beer cold on a bus trip and how to get the advantage in a fight. How best to drink and fight. Hey, what did you expect? My grandfather came from County Cork, after all. God love him.

* * *

I know some of you are not jumping for joy about the previous section about fighting, and some of you don't believe it should be in the game. I respect your opinion, although if you check articles from the past, it's been in the game since the early 1900s, but your side is winning the battle because fighting is going down each year—plus, now, with the mandatory rule (they call it the grandfather rule) where every rookie now has to wear a visor when they come into the league, it will go down further because of broken hands—the visor is killer on hands. And now they put in a rule that you can't take your bonnet off or you're penalized, so eventually the anti-fighting group will have the ear of the league and will win the battle, so to speak.

I wonder if the anti-fighting group has noticed how the stars of the league are always hurt. Last year, we had every star hurt at one time. The stars who people pay to see were out.

I want you to think back to the Gretzky era, when he was flying high, setting a zillion records that still stand and winning all those Cups. Do you remember him being injured? Do you even remember him being "cheap-shotted"? He really had a free ride—a credit card, so to speak. (In fact, I used to have people in the States say to me, "Come on, there's a rule, 'Don't hurt Gretzky,' because he was a star.") Now think about all of the injuries Crosby has had in his career so far. There was no rule in Gretzky's day. The rule was that Marty McSorley and Dave Semenko, they could protect Gretzky like Bobby Probert and Joey Kocur could protect Stevie Yzerman, like Clark Gillies and Bobby Nystrom could protect Mike Bossy. They would straighten out the pest that went after their stars. The NHL governors, in their wisdom, came up with the idea that they didn't want tough guys picking on their stars, which was the exact opposite. Tough guys *protected* stars. Only little rats went after the stars. These governors were right out of touch; the nearest they went to ice was in their drinks (and to be fair, this rule was put in place before the current regime). They came up with the "instigator rule," where if you start a fight and the little rat who was after the star does not fight, you'll get a two-minute minor for starting the fight, five minutes for fighting or a ten-minute misconduct, so your team is short for seven minutes. A seven-minute power play for the little rat who started everything, and to top it all off, if you get three instigator penalties, you start to miss games. So now you can't protect the stars, so it's open season on them—the stars people pay to see. It doesn't make sense.

In the past, everybody was accountable for their actions. If you were a rat and gave cheap shots, you paid the price—as it should be. Again, the stars were protected, the game was policed.

I will give you an example. It was a game between the USA and Canada in the World Cup. Gretzky was going into a corner for the puck. A USA player named Ryan Suter cross-checked Gretzky into the boards, hurting his back. From then on, the injury to Gretzky's back bothered him.

The reason Suter had the guts to take the cheap shot on Gretzky is because he knew there was no accountability for his actions because Semenko and McSorley were not there to protect him. (It was no accident that when Gretzky was traded to L.A., he demanded that McSorley come with him.) It was sad to see Gretzky lying there hurt and nothing done to Suter, but I am afraid it was an omen of things to come. Open season on the stars.

Yes, before the sweethearts took over, it was safer hockey to play. Yes, we used to police ourselves, and yes, you could call it vigilantism, that could be true, but it worked. Injuries were never like they are now.

I don't want you, reader, to think I want guys to sit on the bench and then when something goes wrong, be sent out like a mad dog. If you can't play the game, you shouldn't be in the game. It's not right or fair for a person to sit on the bench wanting to play knowing his only job is to fight. It's no fun, and it is embarrassing.

No, you have to be able to play the game if you're gonna be in it. Dave Semenko and Marty McSorley could play. Semenko got twenty goals one year, and Marty set up

Gretzky with a pass for Gretzky's record-setting goal. Clark Gillies, Bobby Nystrom, Joey Kocur and Bobby Probert were effective players. Every one of my tough guys on the Boston Bruins could take a regular shift. Terry O'Reilly, John Wensink, Stan Jonathan, Al Secord and Wayne Cashman all got twenty goals or more. If some of you are asking, "Why don't they take the 'instigator rule' out?" it's because they can't; the sweethearts would blame the league if they took it out and somebody got seriously injured. They really don't know what they have done, but like I've said before, the road to hell is paved with good intentions.

* * *

I am writing this while in the midst of the 2014 playoffs. Montreal has beaten out the Tampa Bay Lightning four straight. They needed every break in the book to beat Tampa. Steven Stamkos came back from a broken leg; the Lightning's captain and leading scorer, Martin St. Louis, demanded a trade. The reason? His GM, Stevie Yzerman, did not choose him for the Olympics. Martin replaced Stamkos on the Olympic team, and when he finally went to Sochi, he was humiliated. So he demanded a trade, which he got, to the New York Rangers. The next thing that happened to Tampa was that their goalie, Ben Bishop, got injured, so you felt for Tampa. And to top it all off, there was a controversial call on a goal against Tampa that could have been the difference in the series. The call was made by a French-Canadian referee, and then, in the final game of the series, a killer penalty was given to Tampa with two minutes to go in a 3–3 game. Montreal won and Tampa was out.

Ron MacLean made the point after the game that it's hard for a French referee to ref in Montreal, because if he makes a call for Montreal, it will look like he's favouring them. MacLean was just offering some sound advice because, whether you believe it or not, a lot of people feel Montreal gets the benefit of calls because of their great crowds, who are knowledgeable and know how to work a ref. I know it sounds like Ron is my friend and I'm sticking up for him, but all he was doing was trying to help the ref. Being a referee himself, he knows the score.

But then he was asked, "Then you're saying a French referee should never ref in Montreal?" That's not what Ron meant. "If it was in a deciding game—think about it." But it almost seemed like that because of the goal that was called back by a French referee for Montreal. It seemed they just had to put in a French ref to show that nobody intimidates the NHL. All Ron meant was that they should think about it in a deciding game.

If there is one guy in the world that is for the French, it's Ron. He speaks French whenever we go to Quebec. (I think he does it to tick me off.) He always praises *la belle Montreal,* or something like that. He's totally for bilingualism, and it's ironic that now he's cast as against the French.

I just heard a talk show on the radio where they had a clip of Ron and his statement on the situation taken totally out of context. Naturally, they had a guy on who is French and asked him what he thought of Ron's statement. What a setup! This world we live in, it's a jungle. You have to have tough skin. I make no bones about it. Ron and I are #1 on TV, and any time there is a chance to "get" us, it's done, but that is the nature of the beast.

I enjoy it, the danger. That's why "Coach's Corner" is always live. At one time, we tried to tape the show, but the excitement wasn't there, or the danger, which always pumps me up. I know the CBC wishes it was taped a lot of times, and I guess, as I look back, a few of the segments I would do over, but what fun would that be?

I am writing this on the spur of the moment when I see the injustice of this episode. A guy who doesn't have a prejudiced bone in his body, getting accused of being prejudiced. Hey, Ron will survive, and this is not really a big deal. I just wanted to show you the world we live in, but I gotta tell you, it's better than working a jackhammer, and it's the old, old story: if you don't like the heat, get out of the kitchen.

* * *

Hockey Canada. The experts at Hockey Canada who, in their wisdom last year, did not invite Darnell Nurse of the Sault Ste. Marie Greyhounds to their tryout camp for the world junior hockey team. Darnell will be playing for the Edmonton Oilers next year. Six foot six, tough, beauty skater and handles the puck and has a shot like Denis Potvin and didn't even get an invite to this camp. But the best of all non-invites to the junior camp by Hockey Canada was Connor Brown of the Erie Otters of the OHL. Yes, the same Connor Brown who won the OHL scoring title with 120 points in 68 games and was voted the most valuable and best player in all of junior hockey, winning the Red Tilson Award. Imagine: the MVP of all junior hockey not getting an invite.

Why? You may believe it or not—it's political. The way it works out, there can only be so many from every province (the West, Ontario and Quebec) and if you count the percentages, it works out. I predicted a loss because of this, and I am not too popular with Hockey Canada. It's a crying shame that guys like Max Domi of the London Knights, who one day will be starring for the Phoenix Coyotes; Connor, for the Leafs; and Darnell for Edmonton did not get a chance to star for their country because of politics. But I digress.

These same so-called experts put out a statement that they want all kids to have fun and they want the team to follow these drills and they want more drills in practice. And then the experts go on to explain that something like one tenth of one per cent make the NHL (almost saying, "You'll never make the NHL," destroying the dream of every Canadian kid; almost saying, "Don't be foolish—can't you see the odds?") instead of saying, "Somebody has to make it, why can't it be you? Follow your dream. Don't give up, no matter what the odds."

It reminds me of my first year in high school. The school counsellor took four of us into the room and proceeded to say, "Only half of you will graduate," instead of giving us a pump job—"You can do it," etc. He discouraged us right off the bat. Why tell the kids very few make it? It discourages the kids. Like I said, somebody's got to make it. What if all the guys in the NHL thought that way? I say follow your dream in hockey, business, coaching or TV announcing.

I switch now to last year's playoffs between Montreal and New York in Montreal. I meet an ex-Toronto Maple Leaf player and his friend, two great guys who have purchased a junior club. We discuss hockey and the team, and we get around to the practice. So I say to them, "Guys, if we lined up your hockey team and you asked them this question, 'Hey kids, what do you want to do this practice? Do you want to scrimmage or do you want to do drills?,' what do you think they would say?"

They both answer, "A thousand per cent they would want to scrimmage, for sure."

"So, honestly, answer me: in an hour's practice, how much time do you put to scrimmage? Now, be honest."

They hesitate, because they see where I am going, but they answer truthfully: ten to fifteen minutes.

So I say, "Let me get this right. You say you have the teams for the kids to have fun, and the kids have fun scrimmaging or playing, yet 80 per cent of your practice is something they have no fun at. And believe me, guys, I see the practices. Breakout plays where the coach shoots the puck at the goalie from centre ice, he gives it to the left defence, he puts it up to left wing, he puts it over to the centre. Boring hockey, and how many times does that play happen in a game?"

I also say, "I know why you have a lot of drills. The parents are watching up in the stands. If you let the kids play and not do drills, the parents who don't understand will say to you, 'What are they learning? You coaches are just letting them play.' Am I right?"

The coaches say, "You are right on the money, Grapes."

I know a coach who coached a few years ago in minor midget. His team won the championship and every player got drafted except the backup goalie, yet he was criticized by the parents. For what? Believe it or not, because he never had enough drills. Parents are brainwashed by Hockey Canada on drills. How do you learn anything—fix cars, learn to swim, play baseball, fly a kite? By doing it.

Tim—my son, who rates the players for the OHL—and myself can pick out players on a team that scrimmages. They seem to handle the puck better and with more flow to their game.

My grandson Del played double-A and the practices drove me to tears. So boring. Two hours of drills, hardly any net shots, no scrimmages. I had to stop watching the practices; sometimes I think it was better when the dads used to go out and toss the puck on the ice to say, "Let's go," like they did when Bobby Orr played. Same as Bobby Hull. They could handle the puck. Today in the structured practices, where you have to pass, pass the puck, "Move it, move it" is all you hear in practice. How about "The puck moves faster than you"? Look, I'm all for winning. That's the name of the game, but there are too many coaches out there that are too focused on winning games instead of having fun.

I swear to you this is the truth: in the summer, they started practices—three on three for fun in the summer off-season.

I was on time to see Del. The coach was screaming at the kids. He had loaded up a team and played it like a Stanley Cup, banging the handle of the gate for a line change. I call that sick. I was standing by this woman watching. I said to her, "That guy is what's wrong with hockey. What a jerk."

She said, "That's my husband".

I said, "Do me a favour. Tell him this is not the Stanley Cup. This is supposed to be fun for the kids. And please tell him Don Cherry says he is a jerk."

She said she would. I think she agreed with me.

Let me tell you when I became a disciple of scrimmaging. I learned it from the greatest coach who ever lived: Hector "Toe" Blake of the Montreal Canadiens. I ended up with the Canadiens at training camp. I still don't know to this day how and why a confirmed minor leaguer like me was at a training camp of the Stanley Cup champions. I have this opinion that Sammy Pollock, the GM of Montreal, had a very talented team in Ottawa-Hull in the Eastern Pro League. It was so good. Guys went up to the Canadiens, but they were small—as the Canadiens today are small. They needed a tough coach who could still play.

The year before, when I played for the Sudbury Wolves in that league, I had done a good number on their coach for hitting our goalie, and Sammy must have seen I had potential as a coach and I was tough. It didn't work out, but that's another story. But I would have to say that training camp with Toe Blake changed my whole outlook on hockey.

You must realize I had played in every professional league: in the NHL (one game), American Hockey League, Central Hockey League, Western Hockey League and the Eastern Pro Hockey League. I had been to every NHL training camp. I was thirty-two years old and knew the score, but my eyes were opened to new things by Toe Blake. Let's just say they were new to me, but they were the old ways.

Toe was in the midst of winning eight Stanley Cups in thirteen years as the coach of Montreal. Let me tell you about his practices that he ran in training camp—and, from what I understood, during the regular season. Now, you must remember, I was a nobody, but I was treated first class: new gloves, equipment, fresh underwear, new socks, in the dressing room with the stars, stayed at the Queen's Hotel (now gone), violins and all that stuff. First class, not like Toronto's training camp. You were treated like dogs at the Leafs' camp: no fresh underwear, old socks, ate at the minors' table. Montreal was first class all the way.

The first day of training camp, we were given lovely red sweaters with the CH on it in our dressing room. We were a team. In the other room they had all white. We went on the ice; the red team took one end of the ice and the white team the other end of the ice. We warmed up, took shots on the goalies. I said to myself, "This is like a game," and it was. We had refs, and from the first day it was a game. The ref let things go, just face offs (see what I mean? We were working on the faceoffs from day one), blocking shots. We were working hard, but having fun. No boring drills, no stoppages. We changed on the fly, kept score, yelling and hollering—even the old vets. Everybody was into it, under the eye of Toe, who, if you didn't give your best, you got it from him. Instead of dreading the practices, you looked forward to them. No wonder all his players loved him, but they also feared him. They called him "The Bear." Gosh, I was only there two weeks and I loved him, and that's where I saw how a master worked.

I never forgot how hard we worked and how much fun we had. The Canadiens were the best. Unfortunately for me, I was only there for two weeks. I went out with a buddy, Claude Dufore, a goalie I had played with in Springfield. We had a few pops (honest, only about five or six, nothing serious). Sammy called me in the next day and said, "Don, I understand you were drinking last night."

I said, "A few."

Sammy: "Don, we don't allow that. I don't want that to happen again."

Don: "Sam, I only had a couple of beers."

Sammy: "Okay, Don, thanks for your honesty. You'll be going to Spokane."

Spokane was in the Western League. So I was back in the minors for the rest of my life in hockey. But I always remember the master, Toe Blake, with fond memories, and when I became coach of the Rochester Americans of the AHL, I practised the way Toe did. We won the league title and I won Coach of the Year when I went to the Bruins. The players loved it, like I said. I would call an optional practice, and everybody would show up. In four years, we went to the semifinals twice and the finals twice, with a winning percentage of .658, and I was Coach of the Year—all because I remembered and followed in the footsteps of the master, Toe Blake, who treated his players like men, not robots.

I remember I was not too happy when I was told I was going to the Montreal camp. Little did I know it turned out to be one of my biggest breaks. So that's how I became a coach who loves players to play, not do drills, and the players loved to come to practice and played their hearts out. In a game when a player was traded to the Bruins, the captain would take the new guy aside and say, "We got a good thing going here. Don't ruin it. The practices are not long, and they're fun. All the coach asks is that you work hard all the time. If you don't, you'll hear from me and the rest of the guys."

I know as I write this that you young coaches won't take a chance because of owners, parents, Hockey Canada, etc. It is a tough ride to ride, you do take a chance, but roll the dice, try it. As they say, "No guts, no glory."

* * *

I just read that the great coach for the New England Patriots football team, Coach Bill Belichick, says he is tired of all the injuries in the exhibition games and he is going to split the football camp into two teams and have simulated games as he feels it's better to play than do drills. Toe was sixty years ahead of today.

THE 2014 STANLEY CUP FINALS

I AM WRITING ON JUNE 5, after the first game of the Stanley Cup finals—N.Y. at L.A. I just heard that I upset a lot of people when I said that out of the twenty-three players used by the Kings in the playoffs, fifteen are Canadian and nine from Ontario, and from the New York Rangers, twelve are from Canada and eight are from Ontario. I said Toronto and Ottawa should follow the Kings' example and get big, tough, skilled Canadians. (By the way, the Kings are going to win it. I'm going on record as saying that. If they don't, I'll look foolish in this book, but they will.) Some people are ticked off that I said it only stands to reason that if you get kids from Ontario and you're playing in Ontario, the players try harder. With family and friends watching, and if you live in and are from Ontario, the Leafs or Ottawa will be your favourite team to play for. Does that sound reasonable? And I also quoted Brian Burke, who once said, "The Leafs at home have a tough time because so many [visiting] teams have players from Ontario." (At that time, the Leafs, although they are in the middle of the Greater Toronto

Hockey League—which, believe it or not, has forty thousand kids playing in it, most loving the Leafs and would give anything to play for the Leafs—had nobody from Ontario.) So Ron MacLean asked, "Doesn't it make sense if Ontario kids are trying harder in Toronto that the team get more players from Ontario?" It made sense to me, and it makes sense to anybody. The Leafs and Ottawa do have some Ontario guys now, but nowhere near the same number as this year's Stanley Cup champions (if L.A. doesn't win the Cup, I will still leave this part in the story).

This Saturday, I will upset them more when I point out that the Colorado Avalanche, who went from twenty-ninth in the league to first in their division, and whose coach, Pat Roy, will be coach of the year (another prediction I will leave in if wrong), are loaded with Canadian guys from Ontario.

I live in a different world than anybody in the media. I am always with the real hockey people. My son, Tim, and I go three nights a week at nine-thirty at night to watch the minor midgets. We are with the coaches, players, parents and fans. I know what they think, I know what they say. To a person not involved in the game, it sounds so narrow. Understand these parents. They spend thousands, travel mile after mile for tournaments. In doing so, they ruin their cars, cancel vacations, drink bad coffee at five in the morning as their kids practise. Why wouldn't they want their young player to play for the Leafs or Senators?

There was a player who played minor midget who had dual citizenship. One father said, "The kid wants to be with the Leafs. I'll bet you ten dollars, he goes to the U.S. development camp and Leafs will draft him." The kid went to the

U.S. development camp, and *bingo!* The dad won his ten dollars. And while I'm on this rant, let my comment about Russians and Europeans in the Canadian Hockey League stand. Make no mistake: when you have one of them on a CHL team, a Canadian kid is out. It only stands to reason. A Canadian kid whose father and mom have paid taxes, bought equipment in Canada, totalled thousands of miles in travel. I know I've mentioned this before, but it's a big thing with me, as you can see.

After the junior tournament where we lost to Russia, that Russian kid who played for the Sarnia Sting in the CHL said Canada has no talented players and laughed at us. After we give him an education package, clothes, our milk and honey, he snubs us. They must think we are the biggest fools in the world, and we are. So you see, I am extremely pro-Canadian, and in Canada, that is a bad sign. I lived a long time in the States, where their motto is "What's good for the States is good for the world." I don't go that far. I just say in our country, we should be number one. I and my kind want no favours from other countries. Just don't come to our country and tell us how to live and take our Canadian kids' jobs. Redneck thinking? You bet I'm a redneck, and proud of it.

Do you know how the name "redneck" came about? Here's the story. When the Irish, English and Scottish came to North America, they had to clear fields and till the ground, always bent over working. In doing so, their necks were exposed to the sun, burning their necks red. And when the Indians saw their burnt necks, they called them red-necks. I knew this to be true when I worked on construction when I was young. My neck was always burnt. Now, I had to wear one of those foreign legion-style cloths in the back of my helmet. So the word "redneck" was from a hard-working guy who worked in the sun, who loved Canada as number one. He didn't come to this country, take its milk and honey, and still thought where he came from was number one. And that's the way it should be. Because let's face it, folks, nobody really wants to leave their native country. The only reason people leave their country is if they can't survive in their own country or they're persecuted. So they come to Canada and are treated royally: free medical care, free everything, and after receiving all this from Canada, they still think that where they came from, where they were starving and persecuted, is No. 1.

The only thing I can say is, if you love the old country more than Canada, why don't you go back? Funny thing I should say that, because that's what a lot of people do. They live in Canada for all our benefits—medical, health, etc.— for long enough that they are eligible to keep their status and our passport, and then they go back to the old country. They have their cake and eat it too, but they go back, so I'm not complaining. Remember a couple of years ago, these people were living in one of these countries where they had civil war and they murdered one another? We provided them planes to fly back to Canada. They complained that the airplane was uncomfortable and they didn't enjoy the food. Our tax money at work. It costs us millions.

I was told that there are illegal immigrants in Canada living in motels: free food, free health, money to spend, heaven on earth. It was reported that they were very upset at the way they are being treated by Canada. Their big complaint is that they are given too much chicken. Meanwhile, we have seniors living in one room, eating dog food. What I say is the truth. Some people can't handle the truth, as Jack Nicholson would say. That is why some people don't like what I say on "Coach's Corner." That's their choice, but after thirty years, there is little chance I'm going to change now.

* * *

It's seven-thirty on the night of June 10, 2014. I have put myself in a dicey situation. I said about three weeks ago that if we got to New York, "I will dance to a techno beat in Times Square," and here I am, on my way. I often wonder about myself. We have been going since April 16, every other day, and on the road, it's not as glamorous as people think. It's a tough row to hoe, as they say, and here, like a dummy, I go and make it tougher.

We meet in the lobby. Zac, the cameraman, and Kathy Broderick, who runs my life at CBC. You want to know what's going on at CBC, ask Kathy and Sherali Najak, the boss producer. Ron and his wife, Cari, have gone to dinner with Adam Graves. It's hot and humid, and as we walk through a sea of humanity, I think, "You dummy!"

We get to Times Square. You can't believe how packed with people it is—and believe it or not, a lot of Canadians. I do the dance in the heat. The people take it in stride—another jerk in Times Square. After all, they also see and hear the Naked Cowboy. I'm melting in the heat. We get it done, I'm soaked, and we have to walk back to the hotel. I am posing for pictures on the way back, and between the heat, the humidity and the dancing, I am sweaty—and I have to admit, I started to get a little light-headed. We finally make it back. A shower, a couple of pops and I'm going to bed. As I lie there, I think of Ron, having a nice meal with friends, a little wine and conversation. Why am I such a dumb-head? I always make things hard on myself.

June 11, 10:00 A.M. I meet Ron in the lobby to go to the morning skate. L.A. is on the ice at eleven. We like to get there early. We try to hail a cab in the sea of people—again, pushing and shoving. Boy, you have to be tough to live in the city. Ron was telling me he went to a sandwich shop and stood like a polite Canadian and let everybody jump in before him. Finally, a tough guy behind the counter hollered, "Hey, you want a sandwich or what?" You can't be polite in this city. It's survival of the fittest. But I must admit it's a lot safer now than it was a few years ago. I remember when we were here in the playoffs. If you walked along the streets, a guy would come up to you and say, "That's a nice watch you have there," meaning if you wanted to keep the watch, a few dollars would let you keep the watch. Bob Cole and I went on the subway, like two fools. There were eight cars and, for safety, everybody was jammed into one. Seven empty cars and one full. It was a tough, dangerous city, but that has all changed. There is a policeman on every corner. The mayor of New York changed. Mayor Rudy Giuliani had a policy called the "broken windows policy." In other words, you fix a broken window, you save a whole bunch from being broken. Prevents vandalism. They investigate every crime, and they've got tough laws. New York's actually one of the safer spots in North America, but the people all walk so fast, with a detached look on their faces. Bumping and pushing and staring straight ahead. I swear, if a guy fell down and died they'd step right over him.

We finally get a cab. He goes a block past the entrance. We say it's okay. We don't want to tick him off. We get into the arena a half hour before the skate and we just sit there. It's quiet, cool (actually, cold). I enjoy the feeling. We always sit way up high by ourselves; it's my favourite time of the playoffs. I'm in my element and Ron likes it, too. He shuts off his phone. It's like I'm safe—nobody can get to me. I love an empty arena. Ron and I are the only TV guys there. Zac, our camera guy, is there after a while, and other people start drifting in on the ground level. When Kathy shows up, she goes to the media room, where the team puts on coffee and muffins. She brings us a couple of muffins and coffee—she doesn't have to. She knows we don't go to the media room and she is kind enough to do it for us. It is so good, that coffee and muffin. Life is wonderful. She knows we appreciate it. "Hey, you're late," Ron kids her, and she laughs.

Ron and I talk hockey and life. It's funny: Ron knows all the numbers of the players, where they came from, what they did last year. I'll give you an example of his memory. Glen Sather, the GM of the New York Rangers, met us the day before we came into Madison Square Garden and sat with us. I reminded him of the time when he was the GM in Edmonton. We visited his cottage and there was an English bull terrier there. He dressed the bull terrier up in an Edmonton sweater and took a picture with me, which got into the Toronto papers. On "Coach's Corner," I let on that my Blue was jealous. I went on TV the next game and told Blue, "That bitch didn't mean anything to me." Ron said to Glen the dog's name was Watson. Believe it or not, that was twenty years ago. Ron remembered. Glen couldn't believe it.

So we are sitting up high, enjoying ourselves, and I see this fellow coming up towards us. It's the coach of the Kings, Darryl Sutter, and he sits with us, telling us stories. He is just as funny in person as he is in his press conferences. He is an honest, humble farmer, down to earth, a great guy, a super player for many years in the NHL and an even greater coach who has won a Stanley Cup and will win another Cup this year. He tells us about a coach who taught him a lot about hockey. For instance, he told Darryl, "When you are skating around, never just flip the puck into the net. Always drive it into the net, always hard." I told Darryl about one of my theories. When the guys are just skating around before practice, there are some who like to hear the *ping* of the puck when it hits the crossbar or goal post, so they always do hit the post or crossbar for fun. My theory is they then get into that habit, and in a game, they're more likely to hit the puck or the crossbar.

For instance, a player who played for me, René Robert, used to do that in practice, and he hit more posts and crossbars in a game than anybody I know, except Jaromir Jagr. The year he played for the Boston Bruins, in the morning skate he would ring it off the crossbar automatically, just to hear the *ping*. In the playoffs, he never scored a goal the whole time, but I'll bet he hit ten crossbars and posts. Same in overtime.

Darryl sat with us for a half hour. Ron and Darryl are two Alberta boys and they discussed Red Deer and the farms. But all good things must come to an end. David Keon Jr. (son of Davey Keon of the Leafs), who runs press conferences and stuff for the NHL, came and stood in front of us for about five minutes and said, "Sorry, Darryl, but all the reporters are here. The press conference is waiting for you."

Darryl said, "Well, boys, I got to go," and shook our hands and left.

I said to Ron, "How lucky are we to have Glen Sather and Darryl Sutter come and sit with us and tell stories? It doesn't get any better than this."

We leave the hotel for the game that night at three-thirty, as it's an early game. I do the opening and predict New York will win—which they do, thanks to Henrik Lundqvist, who stopped forty shots. Score: 2–1, New York. Back to the hotel, have five cold pops by myself. Ron and Cari go to dinner.

Pack the next morning. It takes me an hour to pack, get to the airport, fly to L.A. Going to meet Ron at 8:30 P.M. for a sauna and a few pops. I predict L.A. will win tomorrow night. I have been correct in every prediction so far. The only thing that got me thinking is Lundqvist again. Still, going with L.A. We'll see.

* * *

It's June 13, 2014, 5:25 A.M. Had a steamer last night, four Bud Lights with Ron and to bed. I said to Ron, "I bet Darryl skates today early." Sure enough, Darryl Sutter is skating his team, the Los Angeles Kings, at 9:30 A.M. We leave the hotel at eight-thirty.

When I had the Bruins in the playoffs, at a time like this in the semifinals and finals, I would let them have a morning skate in their sweat suits. We had beautiful black and gold sweat suits, and we had black turtlenecks. We looked gorgeous. We wore elbow pads, jocks and gloves. They loved it. Why? Because they had been putting on the full equipment for months. I found it wasn't the practices so much, it was putting on the equipment that seemed to tire me out.

If a guy came to me and said, "Grapes, I really don't want to skate in the morning," most of the time I would say "Okay," but you have to know and trust your players. I am not a big guy on morning skates—on the road, yes, because it gets them up and out of the hotel. Some just wanted to fix their sticks and not skate. I would let them.

It was great, especially for the older guys. I had to force Jean Ratelle, who was thirty-six, to stay off the ice. Anybody who'd been in the New York Rangers organization, you had a tough time keeping them off the ice. That organization believed you should be on the ice every day.

Jean was thin as a rail, had a bad back. I had to baby him along. We protected him. The word got out: touch Jean and you were dead, or at least a month in the hospital. (That is just an old hockey expression. You really didn't kill the guy or put him in the hospital for a month. Maybe just a week. I'm just kidding.) But nobody touched him, because if you did, it was not nice.

Anyway, I had to force him to take days off, because for

all his career with New York, he'd been on the ice every day. I remember when I told him to stay home from practice, Jean asked, "What will the GM and media say?" I said, "They won't say anything. If they do, just say you got the flu." Danny (the trainer) is under orders to tell anyone who asks that you have the flu. If the GM asked Danny we'd just say "ask the coach."

Jean responded as our beauty scorer. He was one of the last players to use a straight blade on his stick. I said to him one day, "Jean, why don't you use a blade with just a little curve? Everybody is using a curve." Jean had a great backhand, and I didn't want to ruin that, but I thought a little curve might help on his forehand. Jean said, "Thanks, but no thanks." I ordered him a dozen curved sticks anyway and never heard anything about it, but the next time Jean ordered sticks, the Sher-Wood guy told me Jean ordered the sticks with the little curve.

* * *

I never believed in morning skates anyway. I'll tell you how they got started. I remember some guys always had their skates sharpened the day of a game. One day, one guy just went out, still in his street clothes, and tried his skates. Another day, he brought out his stick and some pucks. He figured, "I'm out here, why not take some shots?" He sweated a little in his street clothes, so he put on a sweat suit. Another guy joined him, and another. Pretty soon, half the club was out there, and the coach saw this. It went from a sweat suit to full equipment and took off.

In the seventies, there were some coaches who ran the morning skate almost like a regular practice. I know some players hate it. How many times have you read about players, and especially goalies, hurt in morning skates? It was nuts, but some coaches did it (especially with teams that were not going well) because it impressed the owners and the GMs. The coach was trying to give the impression, "Look, I'm doing my best." It was phony, and the players knew it.

The coach who feels he should give the team the day off (except the Black Aces—more on that soon) better have confidence in himself, because I have seen coaches give the day off and lose the next game, and the press used the day off as the reason for the loss.

This is a true story. A coach whose team was in the finals had the players come to him and say, "We would like the day off. It will rest us and it will help us win." The coach gave his team the day off with no practice. The team lost the game. The reporters asked why they lost the game, and the captain said they lost because they'd had the day before off and were not prepared for the game. This is the same guy who asked for the day off. The coach was fired. The player stayed.

I digress. The term "Black Aces" came from the Eddie Shore days. Eddie's players used to joke that they had one team going, one team playing, and another team that didn't play and were in the bad books, guys who practised with the team and then again—separately—after practice. I used to joke that Eddie made me captain of the Aces. I used to be hollered at by Eddie more than anybody, so the players made me captain. In the playoffs, you have six extra players, usually guys up from the minors. It hasn't changed in fifty years.

After the morning skate, when the Aces stay on the ice afterward, it is not a happy time. When you have a regular player and he has to skate with the Aces, he will only go so hard, and now teams have three assistant coaches who must justify their positions, so they make the Aces do different drills, which the players hate doing. Imagine there's one game to go in the playoffs, and you're learning different drills. (I know what you're thinking—that it makes the practice new and not boring, etc. Your thinking is wrong.) I used to stay out with the Aces after practices and morning skates and work them. I used to say, "Boys, you are going to play your game this morning. We are going to skate hard, because if you're called in for the game, you will be in the same shape as the guys playing."

We would go side to side so much. The rink managers, when we were on the road, complained to the NHL that we were hurting the ice, wearing it down on the sides. I always skated the players side to side instead of end to end because I always felt hockey was a burst, not a marathon. Besides, going end to end, you could cheat a little. Not the case when it's side to side, touch the board and come back full tilt. I used to laugh—the guys who wanted to cheat used to go to the corners because it was a shorter distance to touch boards. I used to put them in the middle of the ice. After a while, I used to have two guys go together—if one guy didn't go all out, I would say, "Go again." Guys hated that "go again." But you couldn't fool me. I used to be one of them.

When we would go out for the skate, I would have a warmup. "Speed up on the whistle." And then, "Break between blue," meaning skate hard between the blue lines. I just remembered: one day, I said, "Break between blue." I swear a rookie came up to me and said, "Break what, coach?"

I had to play it straight and not laugh. And explain what I meant. He was so embarrassed. Naturally, I told no one.

After the warmup, I would let them play three on three, and they loved it and worked. They would be soaking wet.

I have to laugh at the morning skates now. The guys are so bored. When they get a good sweat, they have to be told the next drill. Like I said, learning new drills with just one day to go, for a guy who is a regular and is benched and put with the Aces, is just embarrassing. So I made sure my guys would be happy. And on the road after the morning skate, I would take them for lunch. And you know, the regular older guys, after they'd showered and were on their way to the bus to go back to the hotel, would stop and watch for a while. And they would say, "There's Grapes and his boys."

I did this with the rookies to show that they were important and I cared for them. Nowadays, the head coaches are never with the Aces. Can you imagine how you would feel if the head coach never paid attention to you? Now imagine how you would feel if the head coach thought you were just as important as Bobby Orr. Well, maybe not *that* important, but you get the idea. We were a band of brothers. The regulars would laugh and kid, but deep down I knew they liked it because they were rookies at one time, too, and they were treated like rookies. Our rookies felt they were part of the team. How did I know how they felt? Because, like I said, when I was with Eddie Shore in Springfield, I was a Black Ace and I knew what it felt like to be a "spare." And I vowed if I ever got a team, nobody would be treated like we were.

There was gallows humour, because we did not feel good about ourselves. In fact, when I was a Black Ace, that's when my anger boiled over and I broke my stick with a crosscheck on the coach Pat Egan and hurt him. I was gone to Three Rivers, Quebec, the next day. At the time, I wished I had killed the son of a B. My frustration was so great. By the way, the reason we all wore black and were called Black Aces was that the sweaters were never washed and black hid the dirt better.

Sorry, folks, I just got carried away with the morning skates and the Black Aces.

Ron and I are off to the morning skate in an hour. It's an early game because of the western time zone, so I will write no more today. I am predicting a victory for the Kings tonight. We shall see.

* * *

I am writing this in New York City at three-thirty in the morning. Can't sleep and am wondering about a few things. The Rangers are down 3–0 in games. L.A. is going to win the series, like I predicted before it started. In fact, I predicted they would win on Monday, June 9 (it's on video). But tonight, in the fourth game, I'm putting my money on the New York Rangers. Why? Naturally, they want to win, but it would be a killer to go out four straight. It would make it seem like they were a failure. You have to win at least one.

(I have to admit, the L.A. Kings have got every break in the series. I know the old saying, you make your own breaks, but the Rangers are outshooting the Kings. In fact, in game three, they outshot L.A. 32–15. Lundqvist is not doing the job right now and Kings goalie Jonathan Quick is murdering the Rangers. He is standing on his head, as they say.)

Another reason the Rangers have to win this fourth game is that they don't want to see the Kings skate around the ice at Madison Square Garden with the Stanley Cup. It is humiliating. I should know: in 1977, the Montreal Canadiens beat us in the finals in four straight, and they carried the Cup around on our ice at the Boston Garden. I remember the fourth game, which they won in OT. Al Sims, the Boston defenceman, was trying to freeze the puck against the boards to the right of our goalie, Gerry Cheevers. The Canadiens stood back and left him alone. The ref hollered at Al, "Move it," meaning the puck. Al moved it, all right; he kicked it to Lafleur, and Guy passed it out to Jacques Lemaire, and he put it home for the winner, and that led to Montreal skating around with the Cup in the Boston Garden. After the game, I said to Al, "What happened?"

Al: "The ref told me to move it, so I moved it."
Don: "Yeah, okay, but did you have to move it to Guy Lafleur?"

I remember after the press conferences after the game, I was sitting alone in my office staring into space, singing to myself, "Oh Dear, What Can the Matter Be?" Evidently, I would do this. I never knew I did it whenever we would lose till my young son, Tim, asked me, "Why do you sing after a loss, Daddy?" I must have done it subconsciously while tapping my pencil. I think the rest of the song goes:

Oh dear, what can the matter be
Oh dear, what can the matter be
Johnny's so long at the fair.

That's what happens when a coach loses. He's always alone. So I was sitting there in my office. All of a sudden, the door burst open and in came Montreal's "Big Three," as the press called them: Larry Robinson, Guy Lapointe and Serge Savard (there has never been, and there never will be, three defencemen that play together on any team. Think about it, two of the three were always on the ice. Scotty Bowman saw to it). They'd come in to shake my hand. I never stayed out on the ice to shake anybody's hand (I know, I know, poor sport and all that). The three guys remembered how I helped them in the Canada Cup that year. I remembered Serge was just coming back from a broken leg that year, and he was trying to protect the leg in practice. Team Canada had an intrasquad game at the Montreal Forum, and they opened the rink up to kids. It was packed. The kids were screaming and it was an exciting game. Guys were getting carried away with the kids' enthusiasm.

(I remember Gerry Cheevers was on my team, the white team. Gerry just hated playing exhibition games, and he especially didn't like playing against 60-goal scorer Steve Shutt. Come to think of it, Gerry Cheevers didn't like to practise, either. In fact, it cost him the starting job on the greatest team of all time because he wouldn't work in practice. I knew that when the chips were down, Gerry would be there, although if we were winning 6–1 he would lose interest and the game would end up 6–3. It drove coaches nuts.)

It was an exciting game and my buddy Lanny McDonald took a run at Serge and hit his leg. (Serge must have done something to tick Lanny off.) After the hit, Serge ran at Lanny and crosschecked him and knocked him down, and all the kids booed Serge. He got ripped badly in the papers and on TV. When I was called by one of the papers about Serge crosschecking Lanny, I said, "Even though Lanny's my buddy and a great guy, he was wrong running at Serge, because Serge is just coming back from a broken leg!"

Serge and Larry Robinson and Guy Lapointe said, "Thanks for everything, and I'm sure we'll see you again in the finals."

So I am laying my money on New York tonight because of the fear of the Kings skating around Madison Square Garden with the Cup. I say there will be a game five in L.A. (I will leave this in if I'm wrong.) New York might win the game, but not the Cup.

Hey, don't get me wrong: I hope they lose tonight, because if we have to go to L.A., we have to pack. I have five jackets, and it is tough hauling them one side of the country to the next.

I just remembered an incident in that Team Canada intrasquad game. Like I said, Gerry Cheevers was my goalie. Scotty Bowman was coaching the red team. During the second period, Shutt let one of his high slapshots go at Gerry. It went into the top corner. I swear Gerry moved out of the way, so I pulled him. (Gerry tells everybody he's the only goalie to get pulled in an intrasquad game.) After the game, in front of the players—who knew Gerry moved out of the way of Shutt's shot—I said, "Gee, Gerry, were you ever lucky. That shot almost hit you."

Think about it. Rangers will win tonight and we will go back to L.A. for game 5. (Rangers won the game.)

* * *

I was wrong—L.A. won in *five* games, but it was a strange series. New York could have won the first two in L.A. and lost both games. The Rangers came back to New York, playing terrible, getting outshot and outhit, but they won because of Lundqvist, their goalie. L.A. got a split, going up 3–1. New York played super again in L.A. in game five and lost in overtime. I have to say, New York got only one break, when the puck lay on the goal line and didn't go in. L.A. was wearing down near the end. The grind of the march to the Stanley Cup is brutal. Those previous series, down two games, down three games, forty and fifty hits a game . . . the tank was getting empty. Some guys were running on fumes. If the Kings didn't win that fifth game in L.A., the Rangers would have beaten them in New York and there would have been game seven in L.A. And as the old saying goes, anything can happen in a seventh game, and the way Lundqvist was playing, New York had a real shot.

Before the fifth game, when Ron and I stood on the ice to do the opening, I predicted that L.A. would skate around with the Stanley Cup that night. The reason was that I had only five suits with me for TV, so the series had to end that night.

The Kings have won two out of the last three Stanley Cups. They did not have a great regular season, as usual. There were times when they were in tough to make the playoffs, but when the chips were down, they came through like troopers. You could make a case for a ton of Kings, but two guys have to be brought out to the forefront.

First, Dean Lombardi, the GM, who brought Darryl Sutter out of retirement to coach the Kings. Darryl had been let go by the Calgary Flames, because believe it or not, he made the Calgary players unhappy. It's the first time in history that a guy was let go because he didn't smile enough. Darryl was on the farm, in the barn, when the call came from Lombardi. He at first refused, saying, "Nope, you have a good coach." Thankfully for the Kings, he changed his mind. The players loved him, but they also feared him. All great coaches inspire respect and a little fear.

Darryl was made for L.A., although I remember—and I'm sure Darryl also remembers—the negative reports when Dean Lombardi said he'd hired Darryl Sutter. The reports from TV and paper said he was too old to work with the kids, didn't have the best attitude, only liked older players, etc. Naturally, all wrong. Darryl's press conferences are classics, and he hit the right note with the players in his speech. He told me about one speech he made before a game: "Listen, if we are going to play hockey in June, we had better win, because I could be home on the farm haying." He is a down-to-earth Alberta farmer who doesn't know how great he is.

I take nothing away from the players. Quick, the goalie, is sensational; Justin Williams was the playoff MVP; Drew

Doughty at times looked like Bobby Orr (I said *at times*). The captain, Dustin Brown. Willie Mitchell, a rock. I could go on about the whole team and their top players, but as far as I am concerned (and I think I am qualified, having been to the finals twice), the reason the L.A. Kings won the Stanley Cup was the guidance of the farmer from Alberta, Darryl Sutter, and another guy in the organization, Mike Futa, who knows how to draft.

* * *

L.A. won in double overtime. Alec Martinez scored, Kyle Clifford got an assist and so did Tyler Toffoli. I predicted in the opening that L.A. would skate around the ice with the Stanley Cup. It was Ron's last time as *Hockey Night in Canada's* host, and as usual, he was the best. Naturally, I didn't tell him that, but he knows what I think. I guess when we're done, I will tell him, but for now we just bid each other goodbye.

Earlier in the series, I did my dance video in Times Square, and I thought there should have been more of me and less action clips. The next morning, I said, "Luba calls to say that her brothers thought the dance was really good." I was starting to feel good about myself.

So to bug me, Ron came back with "Yeah, you know, now that I have watched it a couple of times, I like it. I really like the clips of hockey, except where some jerk keeps popping up thinking he can dance." He got me good. That's payback for a couple of nights before, when, after about our fourth beer, we were commenting about his role starting in the fall of 2014, when he'll be doing "Coach's Corner" with me, but won't be the host of the whole show. "Coach's Corner" on Saturday night and that's it. Sundays, he'll fly to different small cities to do a mini-Hockey Day in Canada, which he will be great at as usual, but I keep kidding him about it. I know deep down Ron doesn't feel the happiest about the situation. Like I said, we use gallows humour. Well, as we started our fifth pop, I started to say, "Now, when you're out in the hinterland next year . . ."

He said, "Wait a minute . . . when I'm out in the hinterland?!"

I said, "Oh yes, that was evil. Sorry, but let's face it, you will be out in the hinterland."

Ron let on he felt bad that I had hurt him and says sadly, "Yes, I guess you're right. Nobody ever put it that way before."

That's the relationship we have. No matter how serious the situation is, we find humour in it, just like hockey players. Sometimes it's hurtful, but you have to roll with it or you lose.

Ron sometimes gets hay fever and his eyes tear up. One day, I noticed his eye watering. I said, "You have tears in your eyes. Is your hay fever back?"

Ron: "Nope." (He never admits it because he knows I would show glee about it.)

Don: "Yes, you do!"

Ron (as tears roll down his cheeks): "Nope."

We were in Vancouver. We had a Lincoln limo pick us up. It was a new limo, smaller than the ones in Toronto. As I went to get in, I hit my head like you wouldn't believe. Almost knocked myself out. You could hear the "clunk" of my head hitting. I was dizzy but wouldn't give Ron the satisfaction of knowing that I hurt myself.

Ron: "Did you hit your head?"
Don: "Nope."
Ron: "Yes, you did. I heard it."
Don (as a big bump started to swell on my head): "It's your imagination."

Never show weakness. Just like when I played. When I got the gout, I never even told him. I said, "I'm limping because I stubbed my toe."

So now the season's over. We have been going every other day from April 16 to June 13, and Ron worked every day. I really don't know how he does it. I can't write any more about the season. My head is pounding and I have to pack my bags. It takes me an hour to pack; Ron takes about ten minutes. We have a five-and-a-half-hour trip to Toronto ahead of us. I guess I shouldn't have had those last two pops. Okay, well, I will write later about the ending of the season.

We meet at ten o'clock. It's taken me an hour to pack, as usual. We take a taxi to the airport, check our bags, go through security. Here's a tip: don't look too sharp or wear a tie, because you will be sent to be patted down or go through the security machine, get lectured—they get a kick out of giving you heck. Meanwhile, a guy with big boots, cut-off sleeves, rings in his nose and ears and lips is happily passing by. It happens all the time. One time, I saw a guy who was a poster boy for terrorism pass by, while they pulled over a little old lady with purple hair in a wheelchair to get inspected. Every person who was in the holding station had a shirt and tie on. So look as crappy as you can, and you'll be passed through easily.

Six hours later we land in Canada and get a taxi. On the way home, we see an accident. A Jeep is upside down in the middle of the highway. Looks like nobody's hurt. As we go by, Ron says, "It looks like that guy is on a roll."

The taxi drops me off first, and he is going to take Ron home. It is the last I will see of Ron till next year. We don't go in for that sentimental stuff—"great year" and all that. We just say, "See ya." As the taxi takes off, he hollers at me, "I still think that dance wasn't good."

I holler back, "Yeah? I'll see you in the hinterland."

* * *

Well, folks, I guess that's it. I sure had fun writing the book. I hope you enjoyed reading it. I would like to thank Martha Leonard of Doubleday Canada for being kind and putting up with me. The part about my old teammate Larry Zeidel passing away has got me thinking that there are more days behind me than there are ahead of me, but I still get as big a kick out of doing "Coach's Corner" today as I did thirty-some years ago. Life is good, and I hope it's good for you.

All the best,

INDEX

PHOTO CREDITS
AND PERMISSIONS

PHOTO INSERTS

Insert 2:
Page ii (top) © Andy Devlin via Getty Images
Page vi (top) © Lucas Oleniuk via Getty Images
Page vii (bottom) © Graphic Artists/Hockey Hall of Fame
Page viii © Christopher Lawson

All other photos courtesy of the author, Kathy Broderick and Leanne Cousins

PERMISSIONS

"It's Time to Speak Out and Save Don Cherry" by Jack Todd reprinted by permission of *The Gazette*.

Contribution from Jimmy Mac to the "Afghanistan" chapter © Jimmy Mac, Winnipeg Corporate Stand Up Comic Entertainer

Excerpt from *Players: The Ultimate A-Z Guide of Everyone Who Has Ever Played in the NHL* by Andrew Podnieks. Text Copyright © 2003 Andrew Podnieks. Design and Compilation Copyright © 2003 Otherwise Inc. Concept Copyright © 2003 Livingston Cooke Inc. Reprinted by permission of Doubleday Canada, a division of Random House of Canada Limited, a Penguin Random House Company.

Excerpt from letter to Don Cherry from Dion Kneller reprinted by permission of Dion Kneller.

Excerpt from Robin Herman's "Don Cherry, You Were My Hero" reprinted by permission of espnW.